Frederick R Wynne

Fragmentary Records of Jesus of Nazareth

From the letters of a contemporary

Frederick R Wynne

Fragmentary Records of Jesus of Nazareth
From the letters of a contemporary

ISBN/EAN: 9783337013080

Printed in Europe, USA, Canada, Australia, Japan

Cover: Foto ©Lupo / pixelio.de

More available books at **www.hansebooks.com**

FRAGMENTARY RECORDS

OF

JESUS OF NAZARETH.

FROM THE LETTERS OF A CONTEMPORARY.

BY

FREDERICK R. WYNNE, A.M.,

CANON OF CHRIST CHURCH AND INCUMBENT OF ST. MATTHIAS', DUBLIN,

Author of "Plain Proofs of the Great Facts of Christianity,"
etc.

London:
HODDER AND STOUGHTON,
27, PATERNOSTER ROW.

MDCCCLXXXVII.

[All rights reserved.]

Printed by Hazell, Watson, & Viney, Ld., London and Aylesbury.

PREFACE.

THIS slight sketch of a great subject is prepared chiefly for the help of minds perplexed with doubts or difficulties as to the reality of the Christian revelation. The author hopes, however, that it may suggest some interesting and cheering thoughts even to those who have been enabled to cling with childlike confidence to their childhood's holy faith. To these readers something of apology seems due. The nature of the following argument and the standpoint from which it is carried on have made it necessary to speak of important parts of the New Testament much in the same tone as if they were ordinary human documents. The sacred name of our great Master and the names of His commissioned messengers have had to be constantly mentioned without the marks of respect we are accustomed to give them. This way of speaking of cherished objects not only jars on the taste of those who feel that reverence and beauty are closely akin, but gives something like a shock of pain to loving and adoring hearts. If the end may not justify the means, it is hoped that in this case the recollection of it may at least explain them, and show that what seems a lack of reverence is only like the holding back of the outbursts of loyalty on a coronation day while the crown is being placed on the monarch's brow, a pause that makes the glad acclamations ring out afterwards with warmer enthusiasm. The love and loyalty have not ceased to exist while the nature of the ceremony forbade their expression.

Again, the author fears that his treatment of some of the ancient documents may be distressing to readers who have learned to look upon each of them as an organic whole, in which thought grows out of thought in a beautiful as well as instructive order. They love to trace the connection of inspired ideas, and delight in the "linked sweetness" of their spiritual harmonies. Such readers may object to the disruption of sentence from sentence and the putting of them together in changed and apparently arbitrary arrangement which they will find in this treatise. Here too the exigencies of the argument must plead excuse. The Apostle of the Gentiles was satisfied to become all things to all men, that he might by all means save some. He would surely allow his letters to be treated in the same way as he treated himself. If they are diverted for a while from their original purpose of edifying believers in Christ, if attention is directed, not to their arguments and exhortations, but to the testimony they unconsciously bear, if thereby some one is led to see more plainly the certainty of the facts on which the Apostle's teaching is founded, may we not be sure that he would say of such treatment, "I rejoice, yea and will rejoice"?

The critical materials used in the following pages are for the most part gathered from books too well known to require particular mention, chiefly from the works of Bishop Lightfoot, Dr. Westcott, Dr. Salmon, Prebendary Row, and Dean Howson. The two latter eminent writers have given to the Church, through the

"Religious Tract Society," two condensed and most suggestive pamphlets tracing out the principal line of thought on which this little treatise runs. The materials for the inquiry, however, have been almost entirely furnished by St. Paul's own writings. If the study of the following argument should produce in any mind a closer attention to those writings and a deeper sense of their preciousness, the book will not have been written in vain. The author has tried to avoid in the discussion anything like a polemical or combative tone. He knows how painfully the sense of the enigma of human life is felt in many hearts, and how wearying is the struggle to solve its problems; he knows how difficult are the questions that press upon minds eager to know the exact truth, and how hard it is often found to answer them. His earnest desire is, not so much to argue with such puzzled inquirers, as to help them to a personal recognition of Him Whose invitation, ringing through the ages, is, "Come unto Me, all ye that labour and are heavy laden, and I will give you rest."

F. R. W.

March, 1887.

CONTENTS.

CHAPTER I.

INTRODUCTORY.—THE SEARCH FOR A RELIGION.

PAGE

Religion needed—Useless unless true—Is there any true religion?—Uncertain answer of science: and of various religions claiming Divine authority—The Christian religion—Nature of its teaching and of its evidence—Character of Christ—Story of His life, death, and resurrection—Witness to its truth in the heart's response, in the world's history, in the literature and records of the Christian Church—A small branch of that literature studied in this treatise 3

CHAPTER II.

NATURE OF THE FRAGMENTARY RECORDS.

Occur casually in a set of letters—Importance of contemporary letters as auxiliary to history—Brief allusions to the history of Jesus in the letters of Paul—Incidents always mentioned as recognised facts—No intention of writing history—Arguments, exhortations, rebukes—History employed to enforce them—Its truth taken for granted—Evident sincerity of the writer—Letters preserved for us from the time when the great movement of Christianity was beginning . . . 20

CHAPTER III.

ANTIQUITY OF THE FRAGMENTARY RECORDS.

PAGE

Four letters of St. Paul acknowledged genuine by believers and unbelievers alike—Opinions of experts—Baur—The "Tübingen school"—M. Rénan—Twofold method of testing ancient documents—External evidence for Paul's epistles—Second century—Voluminous literature—Lists—Versions—Heretics—Jewish and heathen opponents—Age of Apostolic fathers—References by name in Clement, Ignatius, and Polycarp—Comparison with evidence for Greek and Latin classics — Internal evidence — Undesigned coincidences—Language—Marks of distinct personality, reality, sincerity, earnest feeling—Witness of the universal Church 28

CHAPTER IV.

THE TESTIMONY OF THE RECORDS.

Our first question: What did Paul think of Jesus?—Extracts from his letters illustrating the honour and dignity he attributes to Him 39

CHAPTER V.

THE TESTIMONY OF THE RECORDS (*continued*).

Extracts from the letters showing facts in the history of Jesus stated or implied — Pre-existence — Birth — Lineage — Brethren—Apostles—Character—Tone of life—Institution of Lord's Supper — Betrayal — Death—Burial—Resurrection—Ascension—Sending of Holy Spirit—Expectation of return 47

CHAPTER VI.

THE TESTIMONY OF THE RECORDS (*continued*).

                                                                                            PAGE

Extracts showing results attributed by Paul to the facts—Sin forgiven—Men brought into friendship with God—Power for holy thought and action—Life after death—Extracts showing gratitude and love to Christ—Sufferings endured, labours undergone, for His sake 57

CHAPTER VII.

TESTIMONY OF THE RECORDS (*continued*).

Extracts showing the organisation of the Christian Church—Baptism—The unity of the body—The ministry—Godly discipline—Meeting for worship—The Eucharist—Widespreading branches—Moral and spiritual tone of Paul's exhortations to this body 69

CHAPTER VIII.

AN EPOCH IN HUMAN THOUGHT.

Paul's letters mark a rapid advance in ethical ideas—Previous moralists—Confucius—Buddha—Socrates—Plato—Seneca—Hebrew literature—Paul's teaching as to God—Ideal of human character—Motives—Consolations—Future perspective—Beauty of holiness—Moral intensity—Wide sympathy—Modern sound of Paul's teaching—Never antiquated—Highest tide-mark of moral ideas—Mr. Herbert Spencer's definition of atonement compared with Paul's—Moral elevation of ideas not a proof of their truth, but an important step in the argument—Revolution in Paul's ethical tone coincident with his conversion to Christ—Mr. Matthew Arnold's remarks 83

CHAPTER IX.

THE EPOCH CAUSED BY A HISTORY.

Paul's moral energy caused by personal devotion to Christ—Not mere sentiment—Basis in conviction as to facts—History of Christ told in his letters—Two facts specially prominent: His death and resurrection—In testimony of these, suffering braved, toil endured—Difference between belief in doctrine and witness to facts—Bishop Hannington's sufferings: how far like, how far unlike, Paul's—Large community of Christians sharing Paul's convictions and sufferings—Branches held together by belief in same facts—Sacraments tokens of the same—Differences of opinion in Churches, rival parties; one common ground belief in the history—In other religions doctrines the foundation, stories a superstructure, *e.g.*, Buddhism and stories of Gautama—In Christianity, Christ Himself the essential doctrine . . 95

CHAPTER X.

WHEN WAS THE HISTORY TOLD?

Nearness of the fragmentary records to the time of the events—The letters written when Christ's companions were living—Convictions date from long before the writing of the letters—Long years of Christian life and labour implied—Traces of long and stormy history in the Churches—Convictions must have been held by Paul and them from five or six years after the Crucifixion—Scene of action familiar to Paul—The events believed in were definite facts in a recent time and a well-known place 105

CHAPTER XI.

THE HISTORY CORROBORATED.

Thus far only one group of letters considered—Other grounds of information—Not quite undisputed, but of great value—Paul's other letters—M. Rénan's testimony to First and

Second Thessalonians and Philippians—The Acts—The "we sections"—The Apocalypse—Its early date—The four "Gospels"—Their early reception by the Christian Church—Quoted and referred to from dawn of Christian literature—History of facts the same—Picture of Christ the same—Moral teaching the same — Story of Gospels unchanged in subsequent writings—Paul's letters show it the same from the beginning—Theories of gradual development, mythical accretions—Time required for this—Sought for by pushing forward date of Gospels—Paul's letters cannot be pushed forward—Our present creed fundamentally identical with that held five or six years after Christ's death 113

CHAPTER XII.

IS THE HISTORY TRUE?

Recapitulation—Blessings the history has brought to the world—Is it a true story, a fiction, or a dream?—If an ordinary history, never would have been doubted—Has all marks of historical truth—Real objection its implication of the supernatural—Natural resistance to the idea—Result of mental habit—Mr. J. S. Mill on prejudice against the Newtonian theory — Natural attitude towards "occult psychical forces"—The *Spectator* on mesmerism, etc.—Danger of instincts unchecked by reason—Ambiguity of terms *supernatural* and *law*—Mystery of nature's processes, and of our own spiritual being—Christ's history *unique*, but in harmony with the highest phenomena—Need of fixing attention on evidence unprejudiced by theories—We cannot judge as to possibility or impossibility of "the supernatural;" we can as to evidence of facts—That the evidence for this history should arise from fraud, mistake, or delusion, is from its nature impossible—Our attitude of inquiry changed for the attitude of happy confidence 127

CHAPTER I.

INTRODUCTORY.—THE SEARCH FOR A RELIGION.

> "O Father, touch the east, and light
> The light that shone when hope was born."
>
> TENNYSON.

CHAPTER I.

INTRODUCTORY.—THE SEARCH FOR A RELIGION.

IN this treatise I wish to take up the position of an inquirer. Various strong convictions I put aside for the present from my mental horizon, so that I may place myself as much as possible in the standing point of those to whom such convictions seem only dim possibilities or utter uncertainties.

I am anxious, not so much to insist on the arguments for what I myself believe, as to see what grounds those who believe it not may have, when they think the matter over, either for receiving or rejecting it.

The subject of our inquiry is what men generally call "religion." I feel—this is not a conviction, but an emotion—I feel that life would be hard to live and not worth living if I had not a religion. And I feel that I could not have a religion at all unless my understanding and judgment pronounced it to be a true religion. I want motives to stir me to choose the good and refuse the evil; I want to be quite sure that good and evil are essentially different; I want hopes to give an opening into "the infinite" beyond this changing and uncertain life; I want, above all, a personal object to satisfy the "instinct of worship." Whether these wants and desires come from nature or from education, there they are, I know. I suppose education is in some way the result, the outcome, of nature. My human nature therefore is such that I recognise these wants, and cannot be at rest till they are satisfied. And they cannot possibly be satisfied except by what is felt to be perfectly true. Unless I believe religion to be founded on the real facts of existence, it cannot supply me with motives, it cannot supply me with hopes, it cannot make me pray or do right, it can give me neither goodness nor happiness.

Accordingly I cannot help longing to know whether there is any true religion, or at least whether in any religion there is some solid basis of fact to rest upon.

In the language of the scientific students of nature, I hear on this subject rather an uncertain sound. Some tell us that we are able to classify "phenomena," or the appearances of things, but that no knowledge of any real existence underneath or beyond them is possible. "Matter" and "force" come within the range of our observation; we may study their laws, their relations, their modifications, but there all our power of investigation ceases. We are, and must be for ever, ignorant of everything except the various impressions made by material objects on our own material bodies. All else is "unknowable."

Other scientific leaders teach us that the study of the phenomena around us points irresistibly to some wonderful Cause behind all the phenomena. They see a unity in Nature's laws through all regions of her domain, from the grain of sand to the furthest star; they see a strange mystery in her self-adjusting processes, a grand onward march in the development of her power and her beauty, witnessing to a great *Something* to which there is no analogy anywhere except among the operations of mind. In the existence of matter, each particle of which has been well called "a manufactured article,"[*] in the action of Force, the transition from chaos to cosmos, the appearance, in successive stages, of life, consciousness, intelligence, moral sense—in all this they see evidence of a

---

[*] Sir J. Herschell.

personal will, a designing mind, an Author, and a Guide, to Whom Nature owes her being and her well-being.

These uncertain answers of science make my hopes rise and fall. They show me plainly the "reign of law;" they give me cloudy glimpses of a "reign of will," causing and guiding, and dim hopes of a "reign of love,"* overruling and softening the blind action of law. But still my heart is dissatisfied. Can I have nothing but these hints and guesses as to a "stream of tendency" amidst the certainties as to relentless law and the grim presence of pain and death?

Some of my fellow-men answer in hopeful accents that the invisible Power behind the visible phenomena has been made known to men's consciousness in wonderful and supernatural ways. They tell me of religions resting upon revelation from God Himself. And I see in the world various systems of thought, belief, and action which call themselves "religions." There is much in most of them that I at once feel to have its source in men's imaginations, sometimes in cowardly, cruel, and selfish imaginations. Noble thoughts and ideas I see in a few of them, which

---

* See sermon by Bishop of Carlisle, *Cambridge Review*, Nov. 24th, 1886.

make me marvel whence they come and where they received their beauty.*

But one religion stands out from all others in its sublimity and in its direct appeal to man's reason and conscience. Whether it is true or not, I cannot help admitting that it is very beautiful. It seems to promise just the things the heart wants. It tells me of a great spiritual Being, real as myself, though invisible and inscrutable. It describes Him as a Father as well as a Creator, an object of trust and love as well as of reverence and worship. It speaks of His pity, kindness, and tender mercy, as well as of His majesty and glory. It tells of His holiness, His delight in goodness, His stern condemnation of evil. He is, according to its teaching, the infallible Judge of men's conduct, and yet their kind Helper and Protector. He rules "the stars in their courses," and yet not a sparrow falls to the ground without Him. He has prepared a destiny for men after death in which justice, halting and interrupted here, is to be fully vindicated, in which the heart's longings shall be at last satisfied, and the sorrows and disappointments of life be found only a preparation and a discipline for inconceivable happiness.

Moreover, the religion tells me in firm and

---

* See "Religions of the World" (F. D. Maurice).

decided tones that God has made these important ideas be very clearly known. For not only has He inspired men from time to time to teach them to their fellow-men as they were able to receive them, but He has, at a certain stage of its history, manifested Himself to the world in the person of a supernatural Being, human and yet Divine. A Man called Jesus lived, we are told, among men a beautiful life, pure and stainless, gentle and loving, wise and brave. He taught in words that have rung like music in men's hearts ever since. He brought in ideas as to what true and good men should be that have acted like seeds and germs of noble life through all the centuries that followed His brief career. He made men know what manner of being the Great Father is, how He feels towards men, how He wishes them to feel towards Him. He was a Man of sorrows (according to this religion) and acquainted with grief. His human heart bled for human misery. His Divine holiness longed to deliver from the danger, the degradation, the foul guilt of moral evil. The great object of His coming to the world was to save men from their sins. He voluntarily gave Himself into the power of cruel persecutors, and died a painful death, in order that sinful human beings might be forgiven and helped to become better. And still, according to the statement of this religion, He lives. Death could not hold Him. The Power that linked at first the incomprehensible gift of life with material atoms united it again with the dead body of this Man. Visibly manifest among His friends and companions, He stayed for a while, a marvel and a joy, till they knew how great was the nature of Him at Whose teaching their hearts had burned so often, and before Whose majestic life their souls had been bowed with such reverence and admiration. And then, though He was taken from their sight, it was only in order to carry on in the invisible sphere the work of love for which He had manifested Himself in the world. And ever He remains the Saviour and Friend of men. His Spirit pleads with their spirits; and those who will trust Him and open their hearts to His love He enriches with wonderful blessing, giving them strength for duty and goodness, giving them peace and holy calm amidst the changes of life, and the firm assurance of a nobler and grander life after the solemn transformation of death.

And all this, according to the teaching of the men who hold the religion, is not a dreamy myth, not a popular and poetic legend embodying in fanciful story the ideas that brood and germinate in the toiling brains of men till in such fables they find their utterance. The story of Jesus, they contend, is a matter of history. The narrative of His life, death, and resurrection is a narrative of facts that actually happened at a definite time, in a definite place. They find indications of them even in heathen history and literature. Half-sneering remarks in the writings of poets and historians as to the sufferings of wonderfully obstinate people called " Christians ; " a few words of explanation from the great old historian Tacitus as to the origin of this widely spreading sect and as to the time of its Founder's death ; a letter from a Roman governor to the Emperor Trajan describing the numbers and excellent character of these enthusiasts, who were beginning to flood the empire with their ideas—such recognitions they find even in the early dawn of the religious history, half-unconscious recognitions by heathens, busy with ordinary life, of the mighty spiritual power gradually growing in their midst.

And in the society itself which held the religion, its members show us an uninterrupted stream of writers, full and voluminous, up to a century from the date when the wonderful Person called Jesus of Nazareth was said to have died. Thinner in its volume, but even more clear and beautiful in its testimony, they point to a stream of successive writers which can be traced back to the very times in which His companions and contemporaries lived. And on the pages of all these writers, amidst all varieties of thought, language, and tone, they show us the one picture of the life lived in Palestine, the one noble character to be loved and honoured, the one moral and spiritual ideal to be striven after, the one bright hope of immortality in God's presence gilding human life with its holy promise.

The direct evidence to the truth of the religion is, we are told, naturally embodied to a great degree in this ancient literature, leading us back in the historic method to the time when the religion took its rise. There is indeed, it is contended, in the nature of the religion itself, strong evidence for its truth. Many hearts feel that evidence to be so strong that they ask for no other. The very words of the Teacher, as they read them, come home to the conscience as a Divine message with an authority before which they cannot but bow. Nothing could persuade such readers that the simple, earnest, solemn, and majestic statements, the tender invitations, the wise and careful warnings, the restful promises, which they find in the "Gospels" were the results either of delusion or imposition.

But, strongly as such evidence has been felt in individual hearts, it is not much pressed in formal argument. For where argument is necessary it is plain that the force of this evidence is not felt ; and where it is not felt it is useless to appeal to it.

Accordingly those who want to prove to us that the religion rests on outward facts, as well as that it harmonises with inward feelings, bid us study the ancient literature. They give us literary proof of its genuineness and antiquity. They show us how it preserves for us the witness of the men who were the companions of Jesus, saw His life, and heard His teaching. They show us how the sincerity of that witness was proved by the test of martyrdom, how impossible it was that the witnesses could have been mistaken about the facts they related, how inconceivable that they could have invented or imagined them. Thus there is brought before us a series of converging arguments, from the nature of the religion itself, from the beauty and nobility of the ideas it propagates, from the picture of its Founder—too simple, lofty and unique in its conception to have been invented in the age when it first appeared, or indeed in any subsequent age—from the effect the religion has had in consoling and elevating humanity, from the historic records of its origin, from the sufferings borne, the prejudices overcome, the self-denying exertions made by those who first proclaimed to the world the story of Jesus of Nazareth as a narrative of facts which they had witnessed ; from these and many similar sources a multitude of considerations are shown to us, each, it must be confessed, strong in itself, but all united, incalculable in their force, and all leading to one conclusion : that Jesus Christ lived, died, and rose again from the dead, as their religion declares He did. I cannot but feel that a religion so brought before me has deep claims upon my attention. I read various arguments against it in books of mental and physical science. But when analysed all the arguments seem to reduce themselves to one : " These things are not, because they cannot be." Neither literary criticism, nor biological theories, nor theories of evolution, have dimmed in the slightest degree the beauty of Christ's teaching ; they have not diminished the force of the historic and literary evidence that we have the genuine account of His life and teaching given by disciples who proved the sincerity of their witness by sacrificing for it everything, even life itself. The centuries that are bringing more accurate scientific knowledge are bringing also accumulated testimony to the power and vitality of the religion, to the hold it takes of men's consciences and affections, and, amidst all changes of human history, to the firm stability of its institutions.

Therefore I feel that if anything can satisfy my hearts craving for a religion, it must be this religion, and that if solid foundation of fact can anywhere be found for hopes of eternity and aspirations after goodness and God, it is here I must look for it.

I will not refuse all this varied evidence because certain theorists tell me that the "supernatural" is "unthinkable." I do not know exactly what the "supernatural" is. But I know that this picture of Jesus is "beautiful exceedingly." I know that this teaching of His commends itself to all that seems to me highest and best in my nature. I know that never in human history have men invented stories that went against all their own prejudices and interests, never have they invoked the noblest motives of the soul to propagate false and fictitious statements. I take heart then in my search after religion, and feel that it will be worth while to study the ancient literature these Christians refer to, and see how far the records of the long-buried past bear out their statement that in what they call their " creed " we have the original narrative told by the companions of Jesus and stamped with the solemn seal of martyrdom.

In the following pages I purpose to examine, in company with my readers, one small branch of the early literature, and see to what conclusion its testimony will lead us.

CHAPTER II.

NATURE OF THE FRAGMENTARY RECORDS.

*" These are the things which, graven deep on each
Pale line, bring back whole worlds of history."*
BONAR.

CHAPTER II.

NATURE OF THE FRAGMENTARY RECORDS.

THERE are, it is well known, records in the Christian Church, of great antiquity and importance, which give a regular consecutive account of the life and work of Jesus of Nazareth. But the records which I propose now to analyse are very different. They are quite fragmentary in their nature. They are not put together with any intention of describing a character or telling a story. They occur casually and incidentally in a set of letters. The letters were written from twenty-five to thirty years after Jesus died. If He had not died at the early age of thirty-four, He would have been about sixty years old at the time they were written. Letters are always a useful auxiliary to history. They provide some of the most valuable materials for the historian's work. The personal allusions in them, the unconscious picture they give of the manners and customs of the time, the vivid way in which they photograph for us its *dramatis personæ*, the strong corroboration their independent witness brings to the statement of the truthful narrator—all these things make contemporary letters precious contributions to the richness of history, and important standards of its truth. The letters we are about to consider, written by a man named Paul, certainly stand in this relation to the history of the life of Jesus Christ current among Christians. They help us to know it better; they help us to judge how far it is reliable. It is for the latter purpose we are to use them in our present inquiry as to the grounds of the Christian religion.

There is the same kind of difference between the scattered and incidental notices of Christ in Paul's letters and the regular narratives of His life, as there is between the disjointed bones of a prehistoric animal in a bed of drift and the carefully finished diagram of its skeleton by a comparative anatomist. The diagram is doubtless correct. It gives us valuable information. The anatomist knows his business, and draws from his knowledge, and not from his fancy. But there is a sense of reality and certainty conveyed to us by the few bones we have ourselves dug up which no symmetrical arrangement can quite equal. Even so as we read over these old letters, that came fresh from the heart of a man who lived at the same time as "Jesus of Nazareth," as we observe his brief, passing allusions to incidents in His history as to well-known and recognised facts, those facts seem to stand out before us with greater vividness than when we read them formally stated in any story of His life.

The force of this evidence lies in its being so manifestly undesigned. The writer of the letters has no intention of writing a history. He has quite different objects in view. He is eagerly contending against certain doctrines that he believes to be false, enforcing others that he considers true, rebuking certain faults, warning against certain dangers, urging various motives for the maintenance of a certain tone of character and conduct. Incidentally in the course of his pleadings he refers to the life of Jesus Christ as to common ground upon which he and those whom he addresses are agreed. It is plain that, whether the incidents he refers to are authentic or not, he considers them to be so, and takes it for granted that those to whom he writes believe the same.

There is also, it must be acknowledged, such an intensity and fervour about the man's writings that, whatever else may be thought about them, no one can help feeling that the writer of them was thoroughly in earnest. He evidently meant just what he said, and nothing else. The genuine sincerity of his convictions has left its mark on these old letters as distinctly as the veining of a leaf has left its impression on the layer of coal in which it has been embedded for ages. Whatever then be the testimony borne in the letters to the facts on which Christianity rests, it is testimony which, every student must feel, has a very peculiar value. During eighteen centuries the name of Jesus of Nazareth has been a mighty power in the world. Here are letters dug up from the long-buried past, preserved for us from the very age in which the strange power arose, letters written by a man who was born about the same time as the wonderful Nazarene; letters manifestly dashed off in genuine earnestness, saying what the writer sincerely thought and deeply felt; letters by a man who knew all about the great movement, and was in intimate friendship with its leaders. Surely no testimony could better help us to understand the nature of the movement, to form a just estimate of its causes, and to make us acquainted with the real facts connected with its origin.

What these letters are, what grounds we have to know their date and their authorship, and what is the general tone of their contents, will form the subject of our investigations.

CHAPTER III.

ANTIQUITY OF THE RECORDS.

"St. Paul's Christianity was formed by principles wrought out glowing hot, as a smith hammers out ductile iron, in his unresting, earnest fire of thought, where the Spirit dwelt in warmth and light for ever, kindling the Divine fire of inspiration."

F. W. ROBERTSON.

CHAPTER III.

ANTIQUITY OF THE RECORDS.

THERE are many questions in dispute between those who receive and those who reject what is called "the Christian revelation." But as to the genuineness, authorship, and date of the letters we are now considering, there is no difference of opinion worth speaking of. Some of the letters of " St. Paul " are recognised as unmistakably his even by critics who attribute to many of the other Christian Scriptures a later date than is assigned to them in the Christian Church. These are the First and Second Epistles to the Corinthians, the Epistle to the Galatians, and the Epistle to the Romans. There are questions as to small portions of some of these letters, but there is thorough agreement as to their substantial genuineness. To those who are unaccustomed to the study and comparison of ancient documents it is hard to give in a few words any adequate idea of the reasons why these four letters are so universally acknowledged as certainly written by St. Paul. In this, as in other matters where special skill is required, we have, to a certain degree, to trust in the opinion of experts. But as in the matter of Christian documents the experts are so numerous, as their theories and arguments are so widely circulated and discussed, as they are in many respects so much opposed to each other and so ready each to expose any mistake or inaccuracy of another, we can, without fear of credulity, be quite sure that when they agree it is because there is no room for disagreement. When we know that such thinkers as Baur, the leader of that destructive school of critics called, from his place of residence, "the Tübingen school," and the accomplished but unscrupulously sceptical M. Rénan, accept these letters unhesitatingly as Paul's, we can feel sure that the reasons for such acceptance are irresistible.

Critics of ancient literature have a double test by which to prove the genuineness of documents— the internal characteristics of the writings themselves and the external testimony of contemporary and succeeding literature. Now, tracing back Christian literature to its very furthest source, the critics find continual evidence as to these letters of Paul

Next to Jesus Christ Himself, Paul is the most conspicuous figure both as to thought and action in the history of the community. In the latter half of the second century (little more than a hundred years after the death of Jesus) there was a voluminous Christian literature, much of which is still in our hands. Lists had begun to be made of the writings which were looked upon as "Apostolic" or bearing the authority of the immediate messengers of Christ, and already they had been translated into several "versions." At the same period there were believers in Christ who differed in opinion on various points from the main body of their fellow-Christians, and received the title of "heretics;" and there were controversial antagonists of Christianity, fragments of whose writings have been preserved by Christian historians and apologists. In all these lists and versions letters of "St. Paul" occupy a prominent place, our "four" always included; in the versions they are translated; in the writings of the "orthodox," of the "heretics," of the Jewish and heathen opponents, the language of Paul is either directly quoted, reproduced, or slightly paraphrased; the epistles we read to-day were evidently in their hands and constantly on their lips. Going back further still through the scantier writings at the beginning of the second century, till we reach the few precious documents that have come down to us from the age immediately after that of the Apostles, we find the same prominence of Pauline thoughts and Pauline phrases. His ideas are echoed, clearly sometimes, faintly at other times, but echoed in tones that can be easily recognised in them all.

Three interesting references to his writings by name are found in the three very earliest Christian documents after the Apostolic writings—those of Clement of Rome, Ignatius, and Polycarp. To read these may help us in feeling what a strong and recognised spiritual power was this man Paul in the next generation after his own. Clement, writing some years before the close of the first century, exhorts the Corinthian Church thus: "Take up the epistle of the blessed Paul the Apostle. . . . In truth he spiritually charged you concerning himself and Cephas and Apollos." Ignatius, writing shortly after, says, "Those who are borne by martyrdom to God pass through your city. Ye are initiated into mysteries with St. Paul, the sanctified, the martyred, worthy of all blessing, . . . who in every part of his letter makes mention of you in Christ Jesus." Again, the aged Polycarp about the same period or a little later writes to the Philippians, " The blessed and glorious Paul wrote letters to you into which if ye look diligently ye will be able to be built up to [the fulness] of the faith given to you."*

Indeed, as impartial observers, we are obliged to confess that there are no ancient documents in existence for whose date and authorship we have such a clear and uninterrupted stream of external evidence as we have for these old letters of St. Paul. Take the most universally recognised classics of Greece or Rome, put down the number of references to them in subsequent ancient literature, and you will probably be surprised to find how few the testimonies are in number and volume compared to those which are borne in the old Christian literature to the writings we are now considering.

The internal evidence to the genuineness of ancient documents is found in their style, their matter, the undesigned coincidences of their expressions with contemporary facts, the marks of distinct personality impressed upon them, and the tone of reality and sincerity, which it takes such rare genius to counterfeit with success. It does not require to be an "expert" to perceive these evidences of genuineness in our old letters. To

---

* For verification of the above quotations see "Westcott on the Canon of the New Testament," chap. i., sec. ii.

appreciate fully the evidence from the style of Greek language peculiar to one brought up amidst the environments of Paul requires indeed some nicety of scholarship; and in order to give due weight to the correspondence between the arguments of these letters and the special controversies of the time in which they claim to have been written, there must be considerable intimacy with early Christian history. But the ordinary student can feel while he reads the letters, even in a translation, the unmistakable marks of their reality. He can almost feel the heart of the writer throbbing as he presses his eager arguments, hurls his fiery denunciations, breaks out into passionate pleading, rapturous exclamation, or fervent prayer. "My little children, of whom I travail in birth again until Christ be formed in you." "O foolish Galatians, who hath bewitched you, that ye should not obey the truth, before whose eyes Jesus Christ hath been evidently set forth, crucified among you?" "Who shall separate us from the love of Christ? Shall tribulation, or distress, or persecution, or famine, or nakedness, or peril, or sword? Nay, in all these things we are more than conquerors through him that loved us." "I beseech you, by the mercies of God, that ye present your bodies a living sacrifice, holy, acceptable unto God." "O Death, where is thy sting? O Grave, where is thy victory?" "Out of much affliction and anguish of heart, I wrote unto you with many tears, not that ye should be grieved, but that ye might know the love which I have more abundantly unto you." "Blessed be God, even the Father of our Lord Jesus Christ, the Father of mercies and God of all comfort, who comforteth us in all our tribulation, that we may be able to comfort them which are in any trouble by the comfort wherewith we are comforted of God." As we read these and numberless similar expressions, breaking out constantly amidst the arguments of the letters, like white wave-crests on a wind-swept sea, could we conceive it possible that they were deliberately invented by some obscure forger in the beginning of the second century? Could there be this moral earnestness and intensity, this lofty holiness of tone, this warm glowing of human affection, on the pages of a writer who was ingeniously concocting a pious fraud? One of our ablest writers on the canon of the New Testament gives the following strong judgment on this point :—" It is not much to be grateful for that he [*i.e.*, Baur] grants the genuineness of these [epistles], for they carry on their face such strong personal feeling, and are so manifestly not the work of a forger, but the outpouring of a heart stirred to its depths by the incidents of a real life, that whosoever should deny their genuineness would pronounce on himself the sentence of incapacity to distinguish true from false."*

Besides such internal and external evidence for these documents as we seek, but seldom find in such abundance, for other ancient works, there is an additional line of evidence peculiar to Christian literature. The fact of the community of believers in Christ, commonly called "the Church," showing in early times such anxiety to have correct lists, copies, and translations of the Apostolic writings, is a strong presumption in favour of the genuineness of those writings which, like our "letters," we find upon the very earliest lists. The Christian Church, it is well known, was spread by the middle of the second century over almost all the civilised world. There were at that time great difficulties in intercommunication between the branches of the Church, and almost greater still in multiplying copies of treasured books. Nevertheless, with what must be called at least a wonderful instinct (if

---

* "Introduction to the New Testament," by G. Salmon, D.D., p. 29.

nothing more be allowed), it settled upon certain writings, and excluded others, and gave the stamp of a gradually concentrating authority to the antiquity and Apostolic source of those which the judgment and experience of after-ages have felt to be immeasurably the most worthy of such dignity. Whatever weight may be attached to this witness of the universal Church of Christ bears with all its strength upon our four letters, as to whose Pauline origin there never has been the slightest doubt or hesitation in any branch of the widely scattered community. While saying this, I have to acknowledge, speaking only as a literary and historical inquirer, that the evidence for the other books contained in the old catalogues seems to me overwhelmingly strong, and the objections against them utterly insufficient to shake the confidence with which they have been generally accepted as " genuine documents of the Apostolic age, containing the substance of the Apostolic testimony."*

But I think it is best for our inquiry to confine ourselves to these "four," which form a common ground between believers and unbelievers in

---

* Prolegomena to Alford's Greek Testament.

Christianity, inasmuch as both alike recognise them as having been written between twenty and thirty years after the death of Jesus of Nazareth.

CHAPTER IV.

THE TESTIMONY OF THE RECORDS.

> "*Thou seemest human and Divine,*
> *The highest, holiest manhood Thou:*
> *Our wills are ours we know not how;*
> *Our wills are ours to make them Thine.*"
>
> TENNYSON.

CHAPTER IV.

THE TESTIMONY OF THE RECORDS.

WE stand together then, searching into this old religion, upon one solid ground of fact, at all events. Whatever we may think of Christianity, we have means of judging what was thought of it by a very earnest and large-minded man who lived at about the same date as its crucified Founder, and spent much time amidst the scenes where His life was lived. Considering, as was observed just now, what a power that life has been in the world, considering the devotion and enthusiasm felt by generation after generation of human beings towards the Nazarene Himself, it cannot but interest us deeply to see how He was looked upon and thought of in that contemporary age. As we read and analyse the letters of Paul we are going back into the far distance and looking at the sun that has long sunk below the horizon of our own time, but was still visible in its setting glory during his. We shall certainly be better judges of the nature of the life of Jesus for studying it from so close a point of view.

Our present question then is very clear and definite. It is simply, What did Paul of Tarsus think and teach about Jesus of Nazareth?

The amount of reliance we ought to place upon his thought is a different matter, which we can consider afterwards. We only ask now, What do we know as to his ideas on the subject?

A great difficulty in pursuing our search, or rather in expressing the result of our search, is that we suffer from an "embarrassment of riches." The name of Jesus Christ is on almost every line of Paul's letters. The thought of Him seems never absent from his mind. As he says himself to the Galatians, "I was determined to know nothing among you save Jesus Christ and him crucified." To describe the writer's feelings and thoughts about this Person in any adequate manner, it would be necessary to transcribe all he wrote. We must, however, for the present satisfy ourselves with extracts bearing upon some definite points which stand out boldly in his teaching and give their form to it all.

We may for convenience classify them as follows: the nature and dignity he attributes to Jesus of Nazareth; the facts in His life he states or implies; the results he considers to flow from these facts; the feelings he and his fellow-disciples entertain towards Jesus; the sufferings and labours entailed on them by their connection with Him; the society of believers in Christ pictured for us in his letters; the spiritual and moral tone of his teaching to this society.

Taking up his letters then, written from twenty-five to thirty years after the execution of Jesus, we find his ideas as to the nature and dignity of this crucified Man not so much formally stated as coming out undesignedly in such expressions as these: " Paul, called to be an Apostle of Jesus Christ, unto the Church of God which is at Corinth, even them that are sanctified in Christ Jesus, . . . with all that call upon the name of our Lord Jesus Christ in every place, their Lord and ours : grace to you and peace from God our Father and the Lord Jesus Christ."* "God is faithful, through whom ye were called into the fellowship of his Son Jesus Christ our Lord." " We preach Christ

---

* The quotations in this and the next three chapters are all taken from the revised version of the First and Second Epistles to the Corinthians, the Epistle to the Galatians, and the Epistle to the Romans. The words are so familiar to most readers, and the quotations so easily verified, that it has been thought unnecessary to check the movement of the argument by references to chapter and verse.

crucified, unto Jews a stumbling-block and unto Gentiles foolishness, but unto them that are called, both Jews and Greeks, Christ the power of God and the wisdom of God." "Of him are ye in Christ Jesus, who was made unto us wisdom from God and righteousness and sanctification, according as it is written, he that glorieth, let him glory in the Lord." "We speak God's wisdom, . . . which none of the rulers of this world knoweth; for had they known it, they would not have crucified the Lord of glory." "Your bodies are members of Christ. Shall I then take away the members of Christ and make them the members of an harlot? God forbid. Know ye not that your body is the temple of the Holy Ghost?" "To us there is one God the Father, of whom are all things, and we unto him, and one Lord, Jesus Christ, through whom are all things, and we through him." "For the Son of God, Jesus Christ, who was preached among you by us, was not yea and nay, but in him is yea." "But and if our Gospel is veiled, it is veiled in them that are perishing, in whom the god of this world hath blinded the minds of the unbelieving, that the light of the Gospel of the glory of Christ, who is the image of God, should not dawn upon them. For we preach not ourselves, but Christ Jesus as Lord, and ourselves as your servants for Jesus' sake, seeing it is God that said, Light shall shine out of darkness, who shined in our hearts to give the light of the knowledge of the glory of God in the face of Jesus Christ." "God was in Christ reconciling the world unto himself, not reckoning unto them their trespasses." "We are ambassadors on behalf of Christ, as though God were entreating by us; we beseech on behalf of Christ, Be ye reconciled unto God." "Casting down imaginations and every high thing that is exalted against the knowledge of God, and bringing every thought into captivity to the obedience of Christ." "The grace of our Lord Jesus Christ, and the love of God, and the communion of the Holy Ghost, be with you all." "Paul, an Apostle, not from men, neither through men, but through Jesus Christ and God the Father, who raised him from the dead: . . . grace to you and peace from God the Father and our Lord Jesus Christ, who gave himself for our sins." "Am I seeking to please men? If I were still pleasing men, I should not be a servant of Christ." "When it was the good pleasure of God to reveal his Son in me, that I might preach him among the Gentiles." "I have been crucified with Christ, yet I live, and yet no longer I, but Christ liveth in me; and that life which I now live in the flesh I live in faith, the faith which is in the Son of God, who loved me, and gave himself for me." "Far be it from me to glory save in the Cross of our Lord Jesus Christ, through which the world hath been crucified unto me, and I unto the world." "The grace of our Lord Jesus Christ be with your spirit, brethren."

Different opinions may be entertained about the exact meaning and force of some of the foregoing expressions, but looking at them all together, no inquirer can help feeling the solemn, the almost awful position, the crucified Jesus holds in the mind of Paul. He manifestly thinks of Him always as invested with majesty and glory unspeakable. The thoughts of God and Jesus are inextricably blended together. Their names are breathed forth in one breath in his prayers. No title is too lofty to express His greatness. He is the Lord of glory, the image of God, the power and wisdom of God. All things are through Him. He is the Son of God, our Lord, to Whom every thought is to be brought into obedience. Such is the dignity of Jesus in the eyes of this man a few years after He died an ignominious death.

CHAPTER V.

THE TESTIMONY OF THE RECORDS (continued).

*" Before man's first and after man's poor last
God operated and will operate."*

BROWNING.

CHAPTER V.

THE TESTIMONY OF THE RECORDS (CONTINUED).

THE history of the "anointed Jesus," as he calls Him, is evidently supposed by the writer of these letters to be familiar to the people to whom he sends them. He makes no attempt to tell it, only alludes to its incidents as well-known facts. On two occasions, indeed, he stops in the course of his arguments to recall certain important events and to state them distinctly. In correcting abuses connected with a religious rite which Christians call "the Lord's Supper," it was necessary for Paul to remind his readers of the exact circumstances of its institution. In refuting what he believed to be false ideas about the resurrection of the human body, he felt it important for his argument to state distinctly and at some length what took place when Jesus Christ rose from the dead. With these two most interesting exceptions, the history of the life lately lived in

Palestine comes out in the occasional undesigned and fragmentary manner we have described in a previous chapter.

Reading the letters over with the desire of seeing what Paul knew or thought about facts in the life of the Nazarene, we find him expressing himself as follows: "Ye know the grace of our Lord Jesus Christ; that though he was rich, yet for your sakes he became poor, that ye through his poverty might become rich." "But when the fulness of time came, God sent forth his Son, born of a woman, born under the law, that we might receive the adoption of sons." "The Gospel of God concerning his Son, who was born of the seed of David according to the flesh." "Israelites, . . . whose are the fathers, and of whom is Christ concerning the flesh, who is over all, God blessed for ever." "Him who knew no sin, he made to be sin on our behalf, that we might be made the righteousness of God in him." "I Paul myself entreat you by the meekness and gentleness of Christ." "Let each of us please his neighbour for that which is good unto the use of edifying, for Christ pleased not himself." "For the love of Christ constraineth us, because we thus judge: that one died for all; therefore all died; and he died for all that they which live should no longer live unto themselves, but unto him who for their sakes died and rose again." "That life which I now live in the flesh I live in faith, the faith which is in the Son of God, who loved me, and gave himself for me." "After three years I went up to Jerusalem to visit Cephas, and tarried with him fifteen days. But other of the Apostles saw I none, save James, the Lord's brother." "When they perceived the grace that was given unto me, James and Cephas and John, they who were reputed to be pillars, gave to me and Barnabas the right hand of fellowship." "Have we no right to lead about a wife that is a believer, even as the rest of the Apostles, and the brethren of the Lord, and Cephas?" "For I received of the Lord that which also I delivered unto you, how that the Lord Jesus in the night in which he was betrayed took bread; and when he had given thanks, he brake it, and said, This is my body, which is for you: this do in remembrance of me. In like manner also the cup, after supper, saying, This cup is the new covenant in my blood: this do, as oft as ye drink it, in remembrance of me. For as often as ye eat this bread, and drink this cup, ye proclaim the Lord's death till he come." "While we were yet sinners, Christ died for us." "He that spared not his own Son, but delivered him up for us all, how shall he not also with him freely give us all things? It is Christ Jesus that died, yea rather that was raised from the dead, who is at the right hand of God, who also maketh intercession for us." "For to this end Christ died and lived again, that he might be Lord both of the dead and the living." "We preach Christ crucified." "Our Passover also hath been sacrificed, even Christ." "The brother for whose sake Christ died." "He was crucified through weakness, yet liveth by the power of God." "Before whose eyes Jesus Christ was openly set forth crucified." "Christ redeemed us from the curse of the law, having become a curse for us; for it is written, Cursed be every one that hangeth on a tree." "Declared to be the Son of God with power by the resurrection of the dead, even Jesus Christ our Lord." "That like as Christ was raised from the dead through the glory of the Father, so we also might walk in newness of life." "Knowing that Christ, being raised from the dead, dieth no more." "If the Spirit of him that raised up Jesus from the dead dwelleth in you." "If thou shalt confess with thy mouth Jesus as Lord, and shalt believe in thy heart that God raised him from the dead, thou shalt be saved." "I delivered unto you first of all that which also I received: how that Christ died for our sins, according to the Scriptures, and that he was buried, and that he hath been raised on the third day, according to the Scriptures, and that he appeared to Cephas, then to the twelve; then he appeared to above five hundred brethren at once, of whom the greater part remain until now, but some are fallen asleep; then he appeared to James; then to all the Apostles; and last of all, as unto one born out of due time, he appeared to me also. For I am the least of the Apostles, that am not meet to be called an Apostle, because I persecuted the Church of God." "Now if Christ is preached that he hath been raised from the dead, how say some among you that there is no resurrection of the dead? But if there is no resurrection of the dead, neither hath Christ been raised: and if Christ hath not been raised, then is our preaching vain, your faith also is vain. Yea, and we are found false witnesses of God, because we witnessed of God that he raised up Christ: whom he raised not up, if so be the dead are not raised. For if the dead are not raised, neither hath Christ been raised; and if Christ hath not been raised, your faith is vain : ye are yet in your sins ; then they also which are fallen asleep in Christ are perished. It in this life only we have hoped in Christ, we are of all men most pitiable. But now hath Christ been raised from the dead, the first-fruits of them that are asleep." "He that wrought us for the self-same thing is God, who gave unto us the earnest of the Spirit." "He hath said unto me, my grace is sufficient for thee, for my power is made perfect in weakness. Most gladly therefore will I rather glory in my weaknesses, that the strength of Christ may rest upon me." "This only would I learn from you : received ye the Spirit by the works of the law or by the hearing of faith ? " "He therefore that supplieth to you the Spirit and worketh miracles among you, doeth he it by the works of the law, or by the hearing of faith ? " "And because ye are sons, God sent forth the Spirit of his Son into our hearts, crying, Abba, Father." "I thank my God always concerning you, for the grace of God which was given you in Christ Jesus; that in everything ye were enriched in him, in all utterance and all knowledge ; so that ye come behind in no gift ; waiting for the revelation of our Lord Jesus Christ; who shall also confirm you unto the end, that ye be unreprovable in the day of our Lord Jesus Christ." "We must all be made manifest before the judgment seat of Christ, that each one may receive the things done in the body, according to what he hath done, whether it be good or bad."

A very distinct history is given in these incidental notices. The story of the life lived a few years before is told to us who want to know about it, through the allusions addressed to those who knew about it well already. We see in these "fragmentary records" that Jesus was born of the Jewish nation, and of the family of David. Paul considers that before His appearance among men He was "rich," and in coming among men He became "poor." He considers that God sent Him forth into the world to confer a benefit on mankind. He describes him as born of a woman, born under the law. He had "brethren," and the name of one of them was James. He had Apostles—twelve—and among them were James, Cephas, and John. His character was sinless, meek, and gentle, unselfish, indifferent to the pleasing of Himself, full of generous love and pity; He voluntarily offered up His life for others; as He foresaw His death approaching, He instituted a festival of bread and wine which was to be kept in remembrance of Him; He was betrayed; He was put to death by being hung upon a cross; He was buried; on the third day afterwards He was raised from the dead; He was seen alive again by all His Apostles: He was seen publicly by hundreds of people, of whom the greater number were alive when Paul was writing his letter; He is alive now; He is at the right hand of God; He makes intercession for His people; He sent, and continually sends, His Spirit into men's hearts; He is expected to come again into the world: at that coming He is to pass judgment upon men according to their works. This complete sketch of the birth, character, and marvellous career of the Man called Jesus Christ, "the anointed Jesus," is given by the narrator almost unawares to himself. We only gather it up from the allusions that drop from him as he presses on in his eager course of argument, exhortation, and expostulation.

CHAPTER VI.

THE TESTIMONY OF THE RECORDS (continued).

> "*As to Thy last Apostle's heart
> Thy lightning glance did then impart
>   Zeal's never-dying fire,
> So teach us on Thy shrine to lay
> Our hearts, and let them day by day
>   Intenser blaze, and higher.*"
>
> KEBLE.

CHAPTER VI.

THE TESTIMONY OF THE RECORDS (CONTINUED).

WE saw, in the last chapter, the history of Jesus of Nazareth that is embedded in the old letters we are considering. We must see next the results which the writer believes to flow from the facts he refers to, and the moral and spiritual tone of thought with which he connects them.

A few instances out of many will suffice to show the light in which Paul the Apostle (as he loves to call himself) looks upon the consequences to the human race that have ensued from what Jesus Christ did and suffered.

"I am not ashamed of the Gospel: for it is the power of God unto salvation to every one that believeth; to the Jew first, and also to the Greek." "A righteousness of God hath been manifested, . . . even the righteousness of God through faith in Jesus Christ, unto all them that believe; for there is no distinction; for all have sinned, and fall short of the glory of God; being justified freely by his grace through the redemption that is in Christ Jesus: whom God set forth to be a propitiation through faith, by his blood, to show his righteousness, because of the passing over of the sins done aforetime, in the forbearance of God; for the showing, I say, of his righteousness at this present season: that he might himself be just, and the justifier of him that hath faith in Jesus." "Much more then, being now justified by his blood, we shall be saved from the wrath of God through him. For if while we were enemies we were reconciled to God through the death of his Son, much more, being reconciled, shall we be saved by his life; and not only so, but we rejoice in God through our Lord Jesus Christ, through whom we have now received the reconciliation." "Know ye not that the unrighteous shall not inherit the kingdom of God? And such were some of you; but ye were washed, but ye were sanctified, but ye were justified in the name of the Lord Jesus Christ, and in the Spirit of our God." "The word of the Cross is to them that are perishing foolishness, but unto us which are being saved it is the power of God." "As through one man's disobedience the many were made sinners, even so through the obedience of the one shall the many be made righteous, . . . that as sin reigned in death, even so might grace reign through righteousness unto eternal life through Jesus Christ our Lord." "If we died with Christ, we believe we shall also live with him." "Reckon yourselves to be dead unto sin, but alive unto God in Jesus Christ" "The wages of sin is death, but the free gift of God is eternal life in Christ Jesus our Lord." "Whom he foreknew he also foreordained to be conformed to the image of his Son, that he might be the first-born among many brethren." "Ye were bought with a price; become not bondservants of men." "As in Adam all die, so also in Christ shall all be made alive." "O Death, where is thy victory? O Death, where is thy sting? The sting of death is sin, and the power of sin is the law; but thanks be to God, who giveth us the victory through our Lord Jesus Christ." "Always bearing about in the body the dying of the Lord Jesus, that the life also of Jesus may be manifested in our body." "Knowing that he which raised up the Lord Jesus shall raise up us also with Jesus, and shall present us with you." "If any man is in Christ, he is a new creature; the old things are passed away; behold, they are become new." "I have been crucified with Christ; yet I live; and yet no longer I, but Christ liveth in me; and that life which I now live in the flesh I live in the faith which is in the Son of God, who loved me, and gave himself up for me."

Grand results these, expressed over and over again in varying forms! If we could be sure that the old writer had real foundation for his beliefs and his expectations, how ennobled and glorified our human life might become. Sin forgiven, the erring man brought home in friendship to his Father, power for high and holy thought and action, new life after death, an endless destiny beyond the grave—such are the effects which Paul the Apostle believes to follow from the work of Jesus Christ.

We need not then wonder at finding in his letters expressions which show the warmest gratitude, the most reverent affection, the deepest devotion on the part of himself and his fellow-Christians towards One to Whom they think they owe so much. Neither need we wonder if we see traces of suffering and hardship voluntarily undergone in propagating a faith which was evidently to them so precious.

" Paul, a bond-servant of Jesus Christ"—he calls

himself—" through whom we received grace and apostleship unto obedience of faith among all the nations for his name's sake, among whom are ye also called to be Jesus Christ's." "The Spirit himself beareth witness that we are children of God, and if children, then heirs: heirs of God and joint heirs of Christ ; if so be that we suffer with him, that we may be also glorified with him. For I reckon that the sufferings of this present time are not worthy to be compared with the glory which shall be revealed to usward." " Who shall separate us from the love of Christ ? Shall tribulation, or anguish, or persecution, or famine, or nakedness, or peril, or sword ? Nay, in all these things we are more than conquerors through him that loved us." " For none of us liveth to himself, and none dieth to himself ; for whether we live, we live unto the Lord, or whether we die, we die unto the Lord; whether we live therefore or die, we are the Lord's." "For all things are yours, whether Paul, or Apollos, or Cephas, or the world, or life, or death, or things present, or things to come ; all are yours : and ye are Christ's ; and Christ is God's." " I think God hath set forth us the Apostles last of all as men doomed to death ; for we are made a spectacle to the world, and to angels, and to men. We are fools for Christ's sake ; . . . even unto this present hour we both hunger, and thirst, and are naked, and are buffeted, and have no certain dwelling-place; and we toil, working with our own hands; being reviled, we bless; being persecuted, we endure; being defamed, we entreat: we are made as the filth of the world, the offscouring of all things even until now." "We bear all things that we may cause no hindrance to the Gospel of Christ. If I preach the Gospel, I have nothing to glory of, for necessity is laid upon me; for woe is unto me, if I preach not the Gospel. To the weak I became as weak, that I might gain the weak. I am become all things to all men, that I may by all means save some. And I do all things for the Gospel's sake, that I might be a joint partaker thereof." "I also please all men in all things, not seeking mine own profit, but the profit of the many, that they may be saved. Be ye imitators of me, even as I also am of Christ." "By the grace of God I am what I am: and his grace which was bestowed on me was not found in vain; but I laboured more abundantly than they all: yet not I, but the grace of God which was with me." "I protest by that glorying in you, brethren, which I have in Christ Jesus our Lord, I die daily. If after the manner of men I have fought with beasts at Ephesus, what doth it profit me if the dead are not raised?" "For as the sufferings of Christ abound unto us, even so also our comfort aboundeth through Christ. But whether we be afflicted, it is for your comfort and salvation; or whether we be comforted, it is for your comfort, which worketh in the patient enduring of the same sufferings which we also suffer. For we would not have you ignorant, brethren, concerning our affliction which befell us in Asia, that we were weighed down exceedingly, beyond our power, insomuch that we despaired even of life; yea, we ourselves have had the answer of death within ourselves, that we should not trust in ourselves, but in God, which raiseth the dead." "We preach not ourselves, but Christ Jesus as our Lord, and ourselves as your servants for Jesus' sake." "We have this treasure in earthen vessels, that the exceeding greatness of the power may be of God, and not from ourselves. We are pressed on every side, yet not straitened; perplexed, yet not unto despair; pursued, yet not forsaken; smitten down, yet not destroyed; always bearing about in the body the dying of Jesus, that the life also of Jesus may be manifested in our body." "In everything commending ourselves as ministers of God: in much patience in afflictions, in necessities, in distresses, in stripes, in imprisonments, in tumults, . . . by honour and dishonour, by evil report and good report; as deceivers, and yet true; as unknown, and yet well known; as dying, and, behold, we live; as sorrowful, yet always rejoicing; as poor, yet making many rich; as having nothing, and yet possessing all things." " Of the Jews five times received I forty stripes save one; thrice was I beaten with rods; once was I stoned; thrice I suffered shipwreck; a night and a day have I been in the deep; in journeyings often, in perils of rivers, in perils of robbers, in perils from my countrymen, in perils from the Gentiles, in perils in the city, in perils in the wilderness, in perils in the sea, in perils among false brethren, in labour and travail, in watchings often, in hunger and thirst, in fastings often, in cold and nakedness, beside those things which press upon me daily, anxiety for all the Churches. Who is weak, and I I am not weak? who is made to stumble, and I burn not? The God and Father of the Lord Jesus, he who is blessed for evermore, knoweth that I lie not. In Damascus the governor under Aretas the king guarded the city of the Damascenes, in order to take me: and through a window was I let down in a basket by the wall, and escaped his hands." " Gladly will I rather glory in my weaknesses, that the strength of Christ may rest upon me. Wherefore I take pleasure in weaknesses, in injuries, in necessities, in persecutions, in distresses, for Christ's sake, for when I am weak, then am I strong." " Far be it from me to glory save in the Cross of our Lord Jesus Christ, through which the world hath been crucified to me, and I unto the world." " I bear branded on my body the marks of Jesus."

Very great were the dangers and sufferings, and very intense the labour, evidently entailed upon Paul and his fellows in obeying the mandates of this crucified Person Jesus and in proclaiming abroad what He was and what He did. And yet every line in his letters shows the writer full of enthusiasm, gladness, and hope. He tells his own story, as he tells his Master's, not deliberately or of any set purpose, but in fragments of narrative or hasty allusion, in order to enforce his eager exhortations; and it is manifestly the history of a man who so loves this Jesus of Nazareth and feels towards Him such deep veneration and gratitude that he is proud to dare or do anything for His sake.

CHAPTER VII.

THE TESTIMONY OF THE RECORDS (continued).

> "Come, my Way, my Truth, my Life,
> Such a Way as gives us breath,
> Such a Truth as ends all strife,
> Such a Life as killeth death.'
>
> GEORGE HERBERT,

CHAPTER VII.

THE TESTIMONY OF THE RECORDS (CONTINUED).

A GREAT organised society now exists in the world called the Church of Christ. It has existed for ages, and has certainly been an important agent in human history. It is not the purpose of our present inquiry to consider how it has used or abused its powers, or how far the spirit that has generally animated it has been a faithful echo of the tone of its Founder's acting and teaching. But as we look over our old letters written by the contemporary of Jesus, we cannot but be struck and interested by the evidence they bear to the existence of a regular organised Christian society even in his day. Let us consider as examples the following series of passages: "Are ye ignorant that all we who were baptised into Christ Jesus were baptised into his death?" "Were ye baptised into the name of Paul? I thank God that I baptised none of you save

Crispus and Gaius, lest any man should say that ye were baptised into my name. And I baptised also the household of Stephanas ; besides, I know not whether I baptised any other." "As many of you as were baptised into Christ did put on Christ." "For as the body is one, and hath many members, and all the members of the body, being many, are one body, so also is Christ. For in one Spirit were we all baptised into one body, . . . and were all made to drink of one Spirit." " Now ye are the body of Christ, and severally members thereof. And God hath set some in the Church, first Apostles, secondly prophets, thirdly teachers, then miracles, then gifts of healings, helps, governments, divers kinds of tongues." "I am the least of the Apostles, that am not meet to be called an Apostle, because I persecuted the Church of God." "The Churches of Asia salute you." " Unto the Church of God which is in Corinth, even them that are sanctified in Christ Jesus, called to be saints, with all that call upon the name of our Lord Jesus Christ in every place, their Lord and ours." " Now I beseech you, brethren, through the name of our Lord Jesus Christ, that ye all speak the same thing, and that there be no divisions among you. . . . Now this I mean : that each one of you saith, I am of Paul, and I of Apollos, and I of Cephas, and I of Christ. Is Christ divided? was Paul crucified for you?" "What then is Apollos? and what is Paul? Ministers through whom ye believed, and each as the Lord gave to him." "Other foundation can no man lay than that which is laid, which is Jesus Christ." "Let a man so account of us as of ministers of Christ and stewards of the mysteries of God." "Now there are diversities of gifts, but the same Spirit. . . . For to one is given through the Spirit the word of wisdom, and to another prophecy, and to another discerning of spirits, etc.; but all these worketh the one and the same Spirit, dividing to each one severally as he will." "For I verily, being absent in body, but present in spirit, have already, as though I were present, judged him that hath so wrought this thing, in the name of our Lord, ye being gathered together, and my spirit, with the power of our Lord Jesus, to deliver such a one unto Satan for the destruction of the flesh, that the spirit may be saved in the day of the Lord Jesus." "I write unto you not to keep company if any man that is named a brother be a fornicator, or covetous, or an idolater, or a reviler, or a drunkard, or an extortioner; with such a one, no, not to eat. For what have I to do with judging them that are without? Do ye not judge them that are within, whereas them that are without God judgeth? Put away the wicked man from among yourselves." "Dare any of you, having a matter against his neighbour, go to law before the unrighteous, and not before the saints?" "If therefore the whole Church be assembled together, and all speak with tongues, and there come in men unlearned or unbelieving, will they not say that ye are mad? But if all prophesy, and there come in one unbelieving or unlearned, he is reproved by all, he is judged by all; the secrets of his heart are made manifest; and so he will fall down on his face and worship God, declaring that God is among you indeed." "Let all things be done unto edifying." "Let all things be done decently and in order." "Sufficient to such a one is this punishment, which was inflicted by the many, so that contrariwise ye ought rather to forgive him and comfort him." "The cup of blessing which we bless, is it not a communion of the blood of Christ? the bread which we break, is it not a communion of the body of Christ? seeing that we, who are many, are one bread, one body, for we all partake of the one bread. Let a man prove himself, and so let him eat of the bread and drink of the cup. Wherefore, my brethren, when ye come together to eat, wait one for another. If any man is hungry, let him eat at home, that your coming together be not unto judgment."

Here we have a picture very vividly drawn for us, though the artist put in his colours almost unconsciously; a picture of a wide-spread community of believers in Jesus Christ, united inwardly by their faith and loyalty towards the one great Person, united outwardly by an initiatory rite called baptism, and by another ordinance said to have been appointed by the Nazarene before His death, called "the Lord's Supper." The community had teachers to guide and direct it; it had frequent meetings together for the purpose of edification and worship; and it had learned to submit to a strict and solemn discipline, whereby unruly members could be ejected from its pale.

To branches of this great community, or Church, in various cities, the letters we are considering were addressed.

Our last subject of study must be the moral and spiritual tone of the advice or exhortation they were intended to convey. This has already been continually illustrated by passages quoted in reference to the other points we have dealt with. But a few additional passages more directly hortatory may help to bring out this feature in the Apostle's letters.

"A still more excellent way show I unto you. If I speak with the tongues of men and of angels, and have not love, I am become sounding brass or a clanging cymbal. And if I have the gift of prophecy, and know all mysteries and all knowledge, and if I have all faith, so as to remove mountains, but have not love, I am nothing. And if I bestow all my goods to feed the poor, and if I give my body to be burned, but have not love, it profiteth me nothing. Love suffereth long, and is kind ; love envieth not ; love vaunteth not itself; is not puffed up ; doth not behave itself unseemly ; seeketh not its own ; is not provoked ; taketh not account of evil ; rejoiceth not in unrighteousness, but rejoiceth with the truth ; beareth all things ; believeth all things ; hopeth all things ; endureth all things. . . . Now abideth faith, hope, love, these three ; and the greatest of these is love." " Wherefore, my beloved brethren, be ye stedfast, unmoveable, always abounding in the work of the Lord, forasmuch as ye know that your labour is not in vain in the Lord." " Now concerning the collection for the saints, as I gave order to the Churches of Galatia, so also do ye. Upon the first day of the week let each one of you lay by him in store as he may prosper." " Watch ye ; stand fast in the faith ; quit you like men ; be strong. Let all that ye do be in love." " Having therefore these promises, beloved, let us cleanse ourselves from all defilement of flesh and spirit, perfecting holiness in the fear of God." " I fear lest by any means when I come I should find you not such as I would, . . . lest by any means there should be strife, jealousy, wrath, factious backbitings, whisperings, swellings, tumults." "Finally, brethren, farewell. Be perfected ; be comforted ; be of the same mind ; live in peace, and the God of love and peace shall be with you. Salute one another with a holy kiss. All the saints salute you." " For ye, brethren, were called for freedom ; only use not your freedom for an occasion to the flesh, but by love serve one another. For the whole law is fulfilled in one word, even in this: Thou shalt love thy neighbour as thyself." " Walk by the Spirit, and ye shall not fulfil the lusts of the flesh ; for the flesh lusteth against the Spirit, and the Spirit against the flesh. Now the works of the flesh are manifest, which are these : fornication, uncleanness, lasciviousness, idolatry, sorcery, enmities, strife, jealousies, wraths, factions, divisions, heresies, envyings, drunkenness, revellings, and such-like, of which I forewarn you, even as I did forewarn you that they which practise such things shall not inherit the kingdom of God. But the fruit of the Spirit is love, joy, peace, longsuffering, kindness, goodness, faithfulness, meekness, temperance; against such there is no law. And they that are Christ's have crucified the flesh, with the passions and lusts thereof. If we live by the Spirit, let us also walk. Let us not be vainglorious, provoking one another, envying one another." "Let not sin therefore reign in your mortal body, that ye should obey the lusts thereof; neither present your members unto sin as instruments of unrighteousness; but present yourselves unto God as alive from the dead, and your members as instruments of righteousness unto God. For sin shall not have dominion over you; for ye are not under law, but under grace." "I beseech you therefore, brethren, by the mercies of God, to present your bodies a living sacrifice, holy, acceptable to God, which is your reasonable service. And be not fashioned according to this world; but be ye transformed by the renewing of your mind, that ye may prove what is the good and acceptable and perfect will of God. For I say, through the grace that was given me, to every man that is among you not to think of himself more highly than he ought to think. . . . Having gifts differing according to the grace that was given to us, whether prophecy, let us prophesy according to the proportion of our faith; or ministry, let us give ourselves to our ministry; or he that teacheth, to his teaching; or he that exhorteth, to his exhorting. He that giveth, let him do it with liberality; he that ruleth, with diligence; he that showeth mercy, with cheerfulness. Let love be without hypocrisy. Abhor that which is evil; cleave to that which is good. In love of the brethren, be tenderly affectioned one to another; in honour preferring one another; in diligence not slothful; fervent in spirit; serving the Lord; rejoicing in hope; patient in tribulation; continuing stedfastly in prayer; communicating to the necessity of the saints; given to hospitality. Bless them that curse you; bless, and curse not. Rejoice with them that rejoice; weep with them that weep. Be of the same mind one toward another. Set not your mind on high things, but condescend to things that are lowly. Be not wise in your own conceits. Render to no man evil for evil. Take thought for things honourable in the sight of all men. If it be possible, as much as in you lieth, be at peace with all men. Avenge not yourselves, beloved, but give place unto wrath; for it is written, Vengeance belongeth unto me; I will recompense, saith the Lord. But if thine enemy hunger, feed him; if he thirst, give him drink; for in so doing thou shalt heap coals of fire on his head. Be not overcome of evil; but overcome evil with good." "Let us not judge one another any more; but judge ye this rather: that no man put a stumbling-block in his brother's way, or an occasion of falling. I know and am persuaded in the Lord Jesus that nothing is unclean of itself, save that to him who accounteth anything to be unclean, to him it is unclean. If because of meat thy brother is grieved, thou walkest no longer in love. Let not your good be evil spoken of; for the kingdom of God is not eating and drinking, but righteousness and peace and joy in the Holy Ghost. Now we that are strong ought to bear the infirmities of the weak, and not to please ourselves." "Now the God of patience and of comfort grant you to be of the same mind one with another according to Christ Jesus, that with one accord ye may with one mouth glorify the God and Father of our Lord Jesus Christ."

These specimens help us to feel the tone in which the writer of our old letters addresses his co-religionists, and the nature of the desires towards them which urge him to write.

And thus, by arranging passages of the letters according to the subjects on which they bear, we have been able to see distinctly his ideas as to the nature and dignity of Jesus; as to the main facts of His history; as to the results he believes to be connected with these facts; as to the feelings he and his fellow-disciples entertain towards the crucified Man; as to the sufferings and labours entailed upon them by their connection with Him; as to the society of believers in Christ living and working when Paul wrote; and as to the spiritual and moral tone which he, as a leader and teacher, pressed upon this society.

CHAPTER VIII.

AN EPOCH IN HUMAN THOUGHT.

"He who would estimate the priceless service which Christianity can still render even to souls the most naturally exalted must compare the chill, the sadness, the painful tension, the haughty exclusiveness, the despairing pride of Stoicism, with the warmth, the glow, the radiant hope, the unbounded tenderness, the free natural emotion, the active charities, the peaceful, infinite contentment of Christianity as it shines forth, with all its living and breathing sympathies, in the epistles of St. Paul."

FARRAR.

CHAPTER VIII.

AN EPOCH IN HUMAN THOUGHT.

WE are now in a position to sum up and review the results of the foregoing investigation, and estimate their bearing upon the foundation of the Christian religion. As to some of these results I think that all inquirers can agree, whether they can see together as to further conclusions or not. One thing I think we can hardly help seeing, whatever view we take of the grounds or causes of this old writer's beliefs. It is that the general tone of thought, the moral ideas, pervading these letters show a wonderful forward bound in human ethics. Compare with them all contemporary literature and all preceding literature; and no matter how much we may admire, and how cordially we may sympathise with, the pioneers of ethical teaching in the East and West, we can hardly help acknowledging that this fervent disciple of Jesus of Nazareth has left them all at an almost infinite distance behind. We may wonder at the dignity and wisdom in the teaching of Confucius and at the gems of sublime morality that have come down from the long centuries before the birth of Christ under the name of the "Buddha." We may feel—I think we do feel—as we study them to-day a kind of awe-struck veneration, akin to what we feel as we look at the calm majesty of the Egyptian Sphinx. We may sympathise with the thoughtfulness and rising swell of moral earnestness in Socrates and Plato, and admire the calm philosophy of Seneca. But the light of all these teachers pales before the holy glow that burns upon the pages of Paul's letters, even as the stars pale before the sun.

We think of the refinement and delicacy as well as affectionate loyalty in his teaching about God, the exquisite ideal of human character he sets before us, his thoughtfulness for the weak, his sympathy with their doubts and scruples, the noble motives that he brings to bear upon men's wills, the strong and healthy consolation which he applies to the sore wounds of humanity, the grand perspective which he opens before it in the future, so real and substantial, and yet so free from material grossness; we think of all this "beauty of holiness," all this moral intensity, all this large-hearted sympathy in a man who was brought up, as he describes himself, in the close atmosphere of Pharisaic Judaism; and we recognise that the revolution that has taken place in this man's ideas has marked a golden epoch in human thought. It is true that he had an elevating education in the study of a grand old Hebrew literature. Moses, David, Solomon, Isaiah, had left deep traces on his moral nature. But even when compared to these his teaching is like the rich bloom of the full-blown rose to the hints of its beauty that gleamed through the opening sepals of the rosebud.

We are struck as we read Paul's letters by the modern sound of them all. They have never become antiquated. The growth of humanity has never left them behind. Ethical culture, advancing to its highest tide-mark, has not reached beyond them. How could we, who are "the heirs of all the ages," better express an ideally beautiful character than in the language Paul used eighteen centuries ago? Have we gained any moral and spiritual idea by which we could add to the catalogue of graces he describes as "fruits of the Spirit"? Could we improve upon his description of "charity"? Could we bring out self-sacrifice, devotion to duty, loyalty to the great power on high, sympathy and kindness towards our brethren, steadfastness and unshrinking courage in the doing of the right, robust indifference to morbid scruples along with tender allowance for the difficulties and mistakes of others, generous and unsparing liberality combined with steady diligence in everyday work—could we bring out these varied, contrasted, and yet harmonising virtues with greater force and yet greater simplicity than he has done?

Almost unconsciously, the modern pen when tracing out the character of an ideal man or an ideal woman uses the very phrases which Paul wrote in "such large letters with his own hand" not far from the time when Horace wrote his satires and Lucian his dialogues.

We have grown familiar of late with an explanation of religion by the doctrine of evolution. It is supposed to have gradually, in the course of ages, been developed and brought to its present refinement from rudimentary ideas of awe and reverence towards the ghosts of departed ancestors. Eighteen centuries ought to count for something in the evolution of ideas; yet who can find any religious conviction, any spiritual aspiration, hope, or resolution, expressed by the most advanced modern teacher, which is not equalled at least in fervour, in largeness of sympathy, in refinement of thought, by the sentiment poured forth with such ardent zeal yet chastened sobriety by this "Paul the Apostle"? Our highest spiritual thought now is found by "reverting to type." The purest and noblest religious teaching is that which diverges least from the spirit that animates our "epistles." We are thankful when we are brought to the level to which Paul has led. We have never got beyond him. Mr. Herbert Spencer, who, we may suppose, is familiar with the most refined forms of the Christian religion, describes the Christian doctrine of the Atonement thus:—" The effecting a reconciliation by sacrificing a son who was perfectly innocent to satisfy the assumed necessity for a propitiatory victim."* St. Paul describes it thus: "The love of Christ constraineth us, because we thus judge: that if One died for all, therefore all died; and he died for all that they which live should no longer live unto themselves, but unto him who for their sakes died and rose again."† Between Christianity as Paul taught it and Christianity as Mr. Herbert Spencer learned it from Christians around him eighteen centuries have elapsed. Has the doctrine gained or lost

---

* *Nineteenth Century*, January, 1884.
† 2 Cor. v. 14.

by evolution? Whatever then be the cause of it, here is a fact which few can help recognising: that for nobleness of moral tone, strength of moral motive, and sublimity of spiritual ideas, these old letters still stand out pre-eminent and unsurpassed in the literature of the world. Of course we cannot look upon this as a final or satisfying argument for the truth of the writer's convictions. If I am not sure that there is any reality in the idea of goodness, if it seems to me only a pretty name for general convenience, then the fact that Paul preached goodness in a particularly stirring way will not make me believe in the statements he makes. The difference of moral sentiment between him and other teachers is only a matter of taste. There is no use in disputing about it. And if the idea of God is an anachronism, if it is only an archaic way of personifying certain results of experience as to natural and social laws, then it would be absurd for me to contend that this man's teaching, permeated through and through with intense personal feeling towards a personal God, retains pre-eminence in spiritual strength. It is manifestly left behind by all who have shaken themselves free from the bondage of Theism. I acknowledge that as inquirers we must not lay too much stress on beauty of moral tone. I may say that it stirs my heart to its depths; you may answer that you find it tiresome: you may say that other teaching interests you much more. I may admire the Pauline sentiment, "If meat make my brother to offend, I will eat no meat while the world lasteth;" you may think there is much more good sense in the Epicurean motto, "Let us eat and drink, for to-morrow we die."

Argument must be cautious when premisses that are looked upon by some as axioms are counted delusions by others. But thus much we can all certainly conclude: that, on the supposition that goodness is a reality and that God is a reality, these letters are a wonderful advance on all that has gone before them in the exposition of goodness and in the view given of the attributes of God and of His relation to man. This is only a step in our argument, but it is a step which inquirers after truth may take firmly together.

And another step we can all take together without hesitation is the recognition that all this high ethical tone, whatever it may be worth, is the result of the writer's personal devotion to the Man Whom he calls Jesus Christ. It is plain from his eager letter to the Christians of Galatia that there had been a complete revolution in his own spirit from the time when, as he expresses it, "it pleased God to reveal his Son" in him. He had been before a fierce and bigoted persecutor. He had thought that God's nature was such that He would be pleased by cruel treatment of "heretics." "Beyond measure," he says, he "persecuted the Church of God, and made havoc of it." After that strange and solemn crisis in his life which he just touches on in his letters, after he came to look upon Jesus Christ as his Lord and Master, he evidently became spiritually and morally "a new creature." His whole view of God's character and dealings was changed. He became impressed with the largeness and comprehensiveness of His love. His ideal of moral nobility was derived from the generous self-sacrifice and the meekness and gentleness of Christ. The constraining motive of his life was "the love of Christ." Loyalty to Him, obedience to His slightest wish, the hope of pleasing Him and following His example, urged him to labour and exertion. "The life which I now live in the flesh," he says, "I live in faith, the faith which is in the Son of God, who loved me, and gave himself for me." "I take pleasure in weaknesses, in injuries, in necessities, in persecutions, in distresses, for Christ's sake." Mr. Matthew Arnold, with his usual felicity of language, describes this element in the "Apostle's strength:"

"If ever there was a case in which the wonder-working power of attachment in a man for whom the moral sympathies and the desire of righteousness were all-powerful, it is here. . . . The struggling stream of duty, which had not volume enough to bear him to his goal, was suddenly reinforced by the immense tidal wave of sympathy and emotion."*

As we try then, whatever be our creed, to trace out candidly the phenomena presented to us in these wonderful old letters, we must, I am sure, all agree thus far: that the very noble morality of their teaching is interwoven with an intense, admiring, adoring, and affectionate devotion to the Galilean Who had been lately crucified. The world is still filled with the fragrance of Paul's precious thoughts, but it was at the feet of Jesus that he poured them out.

---

* "St. Paul and Protestantism."

CHAPTER IX.

THE EPOCH CAUSED BY A HISTORY.

"*A religion that is to move the world must be based on a history.*"
WESTCOTT.

CHAPTER IX.

THE EPOCH CAUSED BY A HISTORY.

YET another step impartial inquirers after the cause of a great moral movement may take without need of parting company on account of difference of creed. It leads so far that parting may come after it, but those who have studied together up to this cannot well stop short of it. We have seen that affectionate devotion to Jesus Christ was the principal factor in the moral energy of the writer of our letters. But this affection was not a mere sentimental affection, not merely a union caused by sympathy of souls. It had its basis in a firm conviction as to certain matters of fact. We perceived, as we studied the letters, the synopsis of the history of "Jesus" that they almost unconsciously give us. As the author writes on various subjects, he cannot help telling the story that occupied so large a place in his own thoughts. We saw specially marked on every page of them the prominence in Paul's mind of two events that evidently seemed to him to be of the most vital significance : the death and the resurrection of Jesus Christ. He connected with that death momentous consequences for all humanity; he saw in that resurrection the opening of an infinite vista of hope for man's futurity. Whether we agree or disagree as to his ideas with regard to the facts, we must agree that he believed them, and believed them both equally; we must agree that he was thoroughly persuaded that Jesus Christ died and rose again ; and that this persuasion was the ground of all the convictions, feelings, and actions described in his letters. That Jesus of Nazareth was a supernatural Being, that He lived a supernatural life, that He voluntarily died to save mankind, that He rose again after death nevermore to die, that He was in some real and awful sense a manifestation to man of the glorious, invisible God—this undoubtedly was the firm belief of Paul ; this was the foundation of his faith and devotion, the ground upon which he rested his ethical teaching. It is impossible to study the man's letters without being sure of this.

And his certainty about these facts was so

strong that he braved all kinds of persecution in his proclamation of them. He lived a life of hardship, suffering, and danger. For long years, as appears plainly in his letters, he had no rest, travelling by sea and land, assaulted with savage fury both by Jews and heathens, beaten, stoned, and even made to fight for his life with wild beasts, all because he believed it to be his bounden duty to make known everywhere that Jesus Christ had risen from the dead, and was " the Son of God." Brave and devoted men go through similar hardships still from a similar cause. The late Bishop Hannington in his "journeyings often" through fever-stricken jungle, in his "perils by waters," "perils by robbers," in his captivity, loneliness, and savage execution, went through the same kind of experience as Paul did. The cause is the same : intense conviction of the truth of the Christian creed. In the modern and in the ancient missionary alike we see the indomitable force given by faith in the risen Jesus. We admire the modern devotion. It teaches us the power of strong conviction, the grandeur of a holy enthusiasm, the almost superhuman beauty of character still produced by communion of soul with Jesus of Nazareth. But in the old missionary devotion we see something even more significant—the persuasion as to facts of one who lived at the time the facts took place. It is not Paul's nobility, Paul's self-sacrifice, Paul's courage and burning zeal, which rivets our attention; it is Paul's firm certainty and unshaken testimony as to events which he believed to have happened in his own age and in his own country.

And sharing both his convictions and sufferings, we see described in the "letters," as we have just now noticed, a community born in the throes of persecution, yet already large, its branches spread over many lands, but knit very closely one to another, helping and supporting each other, acknowledging the same spiritual government, and submitting to a sharp, strong discipline. The letters refer or allude to its members in Judæa, Jerusalem, Antioch, Damascus, Galatia, Ephesus, Macedonia, Achaia, Cenchrea, and Rome. They were held together by their belief in the same facts that Paul believed in. They practised certain outward rites as tokens, signs, and seals, visible to the world, of the truths their hearts rested in. Thus the letters present to us not only one man enthusiastically holding certain convictions, but a great organised body of men and women, spread throughout the civilised world, believing the same as he did. To the zeal and energy of this man no doubt many of the branch communities owed their birth. But several received their faith from sources independent of him. He was "unknown by face to the Churches of Judæa which were in Christ; they only heard say, 'He that once persecuted us now preacheth the faith of which he once made havoc.'" He had never been at Rome, though for many years he had had a longing to come to them.* For many years before he wrote his letter to them there had been believers in Jesus Christ there with whom he had as yet had no communication. Two at least of these had been "in Christ" before him.† Among the members of the Churches there had sprung up from time to time great differences of opinion, rival parties, rival leaders and teachers. Some of the parties were bitterly opposed to Paul himself, and evidently made little of his authority. He is obliged, at the risk of seeming egotistic, to vindicate his apostleship from their charges.‡

---

* Gal. i. 22, 23 ; Rom. xv. 23.

† Rom. xvi. 7. This is the only reference I make to the sixteenth chapter of Romans, because, thoroughly genuine as I believe it to be, there is not quite the same unanimity of critical opinion with regard to it as to the rest of the Epistle.

‡ See 2 Cor. x., xi., xii.

But whatever may have been their differences as to theoretic views or as to favourite teachers, there was always one common ground between them: their belief in the same history of facts. In arguing with them, rebuking, persuading, or warning, Paul could appeal to this without fear of contradiction. It was the standing ground of all alike. Some professing Christians, for example, denied the resurrection of the body. Paul showed the unreasonableness of their views, not by abstract arguments, but by the fact of Christ's resurrection. "If resurrection is impossible," he says, "Christ could not have risen. And if Christ has not risen, our preaching is vain, and your faith is vain." He does not say, "Resurrection is possible, resurrection is likely, so you may believe that Christ rose." But he says, "You know that Christ rose, so it is absurd to suppose that resurrection is impossible." He refutes the vague theory by the acknowledged fact. In other systems of religion, doctrines, philosophical or spiritual, form the foundation, stories as to the founder's life only a light and somewhat ornamental superstructure. With the Confucian the great thing is the "Tao"—doctrine, principle, way of living—the history of Confucius himself is nothing.

In the religion of Buddha, which has come rather prominently before European notice of late, and which has been painted for us in such beautiful colours by Mr. Edwin Arnold's poetic genius,* the sublime thing which we wonder at is the pure and noble, though somewhat frigid, moral teaching of the great recluse. The story of Gautama, though variously told, seems to have a solid substratum of fact, but it is embellished at different times, after the lapse of centuries, by different hands with accretions of mythic legends. They are not, however, the religion; they are only a floating drapery thrown around it by friendly hands to enhance its beauty. Take away the drapery, and the essence of the religion is unaffected. It is very different with the religion we are inquiring into now. The great doctrine of Christianity is Christ Himself. What Paul went about preaching so earnestly was Christ crucified. He was determined to know nothing among his hearers but that alone. Jesus and the Resurrection was the great fulcrum on which all his moral exhortation rested. Eliminate from his teaching the story of facts about the dead and risen Jesus, and he has no message to give, no doctrine to declare. The

---

* "The Light of Asia." By E. Arnold.

Church whose wide ramifications and strong organisation appears before us in these letters was built upon " one foundation." "None other," says Paul, "can any man lay than that which is laid, which is Christ Jesus."

Thus we have, photographed for us in these letters, a wide-spread society, holding its ground firmly against persecution, imbued with the most beautiful ethical ideas, and resting for its existence on the common conviction that Jesus of Nazareth was the Son of God, and had risen from the dead.

CHAPTER X.

WHEN WAS THE HISTORY TOLD?

*"Oh, bright and happy Kalendar
Where youth shines like a star
All pearl'd with tears, and may
Teach age the Holy way;
When through thick pangs, high agonies,
Faith unto life breaks, and death dies."*
                                        HENRY VAUGHAN.

CHAPTER X.

WHEN WAS THE HISTORY TOLD?

THE picture of the Church bound together by strong conviction as to the truth of a history of facts, which we have been studying, was drawn, let us keep well in mind, certainly within thirty years after the Nazarene had been crucified. If He had lived, He would have been, as we noticed in a previous chapter, about sixty years of age when the latest of these letters was written. His companions were still living. John, Peter, and "James the Less" were evidently alive at the time they were spoken of in the letter to the Galatians. When the letter to the Corinthians was penned, the writer distinctly tells us that of above five hundred brethren to whom Christ appeared after His resurrection, the greater part still remained. The "Apostles," or principal friends and personal companions of Christ, with whom the writer of our letters was evidently intimate, with whom he had many communications, with one of whom, we know, he had stayed in consultation for fifteen days, " gave him the right hand of fellowship," and were thoroughly in agreement with him as to the history of Jesus, though on a point of practical detail he tells us he had a sharp difference of opinion with one of them.

In the convictions of Paul, then, when he wrote these letters, in the agreement concerning them among the several branches of the Christian Church, in the assent to them given by those best qualified to know the actual facts of the case, we certainly have a very near view of the great Figure, Who had so lately disappeared.

But the letters when carefully considered bring us back to a period even nearer the life of Christ than the date at which they were written. The stately galleon has taken in its cargo at a point much higher up the river than where first we see it sweeping down to the sea. The convictions expressed by the writer twenty-five or twenty-eight years after the death of " Jesus " were evidently convictions that he had long held. He describes a course of labour which may almost be called a lifelong labour. " In prisons abundantly, in stripes above measure, in deaths oft," five times scourged with the forty stripes save one, thrice beaten with rods, once stoned, thrice shipwrecked, in journeyings often, in perils of rivers, of robbers, of Jews, of Gentiles, in perils in the city, in the wilderness, in the sea, among false brethren, in labour and travail, in watchings often, in hunger and thirst, in fastings often, in cold and nakedness, — such were his experiences. They were the experiences of a long career of hardship. He tells us that three years elapsed between his conversion and his return to Jerusalem, and then fourteen years before he visited it again. These little sentences help us to realise what indeed is implied in the whole tone of his letters: that it was no new gospel he was preaching, but a faith of whose truth he had been intensely convinced for a long course of years. And the communities to which he wrote had also manifestly held the same belief for a considerable period of time, long enough to allow divisions and parties to spring up, grow, and ripen among them. The Churches of Galatia and of Corinth had been planted by him, and since their planting they had each had a stormy and eventful history. The Church in Rome had been pursuing its career so as to interest him and draw out his sympathy for "many years." The Churches of Judæa were believers in Jesus Christ before he was. The ideas then that were common to him and to the branches of the Christian Church which his letters bring into sight were ideas which he must have held for twenty years at the very lowest computation.

Our hearts must thrill with a sense of very solemn interest when we realise to ourselves what this implies. We can read to-day the sentiments and ideas entertained about Jesus Christ by a most earnest and able man five or six years, or probably even less, after He had disappeared from the world. This is no guesswork. We have the letters in our hands. They are as fresh and lifelike as if the ink with which they were written were hardly dried. The writer is so warm and frank and earnest that we cannot help knowing exactly what he thought and felt about that which seemed to him a subject of life-or-death interest for all humanity. We know by the surest results of historical and literary history exactly the date within two or three years at least when the letters were written. We have plain tokens that the convictions expressed were embraced twenty years before. So we know with absolute certainty what Saul of Tarsus and the many co-religionists of Saul of Tarsus thought about Jesus of Nazareth five or six years after His death. At that period the story of Jesus, whatever it may have been, was, at all events, quite fresh in people's minds. There had been no time yet for a halo of mythic sanctity to crown the heads of the actors in the drama. They were most of them still living. They were evidently busy and active, declaring the story and guiding the community that had just been formed on the basis of it. When Paul was won to the faith which, as he tells us, he used to persecute, everything about Jesus Christ was distinct in the clearness of a recent date and a familiar scene of action. Every spot in that little country of Palestine was doubtless known to him. As he speaks to John and James and spends weeks with Peter, who had all been lately going about with Jesus, there are, at all events, no dreamy mists of long-past ages and distant lands to rise up between him and the object of his convictions and blur its outlines with vague and poetic traditions. The revolution in his lifelong habits of thought proceeds from his persuasion of the truth of a few definite facts easily tested. Whether he was right or wrong in his persuasion, it is plain that his judgment had to be exercised upon recent events, and not upon old fables.

CHAPTER XI.

CORROBORATION OF THE HISTORY.

> "Were knowledge all thy faculty, then God
> Must be ignored, love gains Him by first leap."
>
> BROWNING.

CHAPTER XI.

CORROBORATIVE EVIDENCE TO THE HISTORY.

THUS far, according to the design of this discussion, we have confined our attention entirely to one little group of letters. It is but a very small field for research amidst the voluminous literature connected with the important subject of our inquiry. But it has had the advantage of being thoroughly solid ground. We all, whether we believe or doubt the Christian religion, believe in the genuineness and early date of these letters. The conclusions we have hitherto drawn are, I believe, speaking only as an inquirer, almost beyond controversy. The feelings of Paul and his fellow-Christians towards Jesus of Nazareth; their convictions and ideas about His history; the sufferings they underwent in behalf of their testimony; the nearness of the time when they thus thought and felt and suffered to the events in which they believed—all this is certainly made plain to us in what Paul so certainly wrote during the lifetime of " Christ's " companions.

But it is well that we should be reminded at this point in our inquiries that the letters we have been considering are not our only sources of information with regard to Jesus of Nazareth. There are others which, though not, like these, absolutely undisputed, are yet of very reliable authority. It does not fall within the scope of our present discussion to review them at any length. But it would be an injustice to our argument if we were to forget or ignore the various branches of Christian literature which run parallel with that which we have been considering, and both give to it and receive from it important support. There are a number of letters of Paul's not unanimously received by ingenious German critics, but confidently accepted by the universal community of Christians from the earliest date at which we can distinguish its voice. Of some of these (the Epistle to the Philippians and two Epistles to the Thessalonians) even M. Rénan says that the objections made against them are only "light suspicions which criticism ought not to stop at when stronger reasons bear it onward." The letters, he says, "have a character of authenticity which overcomes every other consideration."* Besides these and interesting letters by other hands whose claims to our confidence we cannot here discuss, the community of Christians have guarded with jealous care several writings of a different kind, which they believed to have emanated from about the same date as Paul's letters. There is a history called "The Acts of the Apostles," named among the Apostolic writings in the Muratorian fragment (A.D. 170), quoted continually and copiously in the latter part of the second century, referred to apparently by many of the very earliest Christian writers. The concluding portion of this book contains a detailed history of some of Paul's missionary journeys. The parts of it called the "*we* sections" are acknowledged even by the "Tübingen school" to be the genuine records of an eyewitness. M. Rénan admits them to form "an entirely historical narrative."

There is also a strange book written in mystic language hard to be deciphered in the present day, but containing bursts of lofty eloquence which have echoed ever since in the hymns of the Christian Church, and flashes of splendid description which have given colour and warmth

---

* Rénan, St. Paul, Introduction, p. vi.

to her poetry and her art from generation to generation. This book is now recognised by the general voice of criticism to date from a very few years after the crucifixion of Jesus. In all these writings—letters, history, mystic allegory—we have exactly the same testimony to the subject of our inquiry as we have seen borne by the old letters we have studied. We have the same personal picture of the great Figure Who is held up for adoration, confidence, and love; the same lofty, unselfish, yet plain and practical moral teaching, vivified by the same intense motives of affection and loyalty to the great God and to the Saviour Jesus Christ; the same history of facts implied or expressed—the history of Jesus Christ living, dying, rising again " for us men and for our salvation." As to the essentials of faith and feeling, we find perfect unanimity with Paul's letters in all these ancient documents.

But there are others still, if possible, more important. We have found in our letters fragmentary and undesigned records of Jesus. But there are four regular histories, drawn up with great care, giving in close detail what we have only seen hitherto in rough and general sketch. They are very ancient documents. They have been unanimously received by the Christian Church as written in Apostolic times and coming to us with Apostolic authority. They are mentioned in the old catalogue we have spoken of; they are tabulated in harmony by a writer early in the second century; they are quoted and requoted and made the basis of argument by rival sects of Christians and opponents of Christianity, from the very dawn of Christian literature.

How do these orderly histories stand towards our fragmentary records? Do they tell the same or a different story? Can we recognise in them the same countenance that gleams out so beautifully through the hurried and blotted characters of the letters?

The answer is not hard to give. Take the several points in the life of Jesus which we saw mentioned or implied in the letters; they are all distinctly set down in the histories. Take the features in His character, the great hopes and beliefs and motives to holy living which Paul makes the ground of his reasonings and expostulations with his readers; we find them all in the plain narratives of His sayings and doings. In the fervent rhetoric of the letter-writer there is described to us a lofty ideal of human goodness; in the calmly told narrative of the "Gospel" this ideal stands out before us, a living model so majestic that we bow down before it in admiration, so warm and human that we take it to our hearts in close personal affection. As we read " St. Paul's epistles " we are pressed to think of whatsoever things are pure, lovely, and of good report; we are led to long and pray for " love, joy, peace, longsuffering, kindness, goodness, faithfulness, meekness, temperance." As we read the Gospels we see these graces acted out before our eyes : we see the strong, patient figure of the Nazarene ; we see Him spending His whole life for the good of others ; we see Him set upon the one great purpose of doing duty, doing His Father's will ; we see a strength of determination so unswerving, and yet so devoid of self-consciousness that, like the great sweep of the earth in her orbit, its movement is hardly noticed. We see thoughtfulness, kindness, gentle sympathy, merciful help : arms that took the little children and folded them to His breast ; hands that touched the loathsome leper, and lifted the sick and dying from their beds ; eyes that never quailed before human opposition, threats, or scorn, but were often enough dimmed with tears for human sorrow. We listen to His teaching, and find in it the clear voice of which Paul's exhortations are the ringing echo. We hear His simple parables for the poor, His loving consolations to His disciples, His thunders of scorn and wrath for Pharisees and hypocrites. Here are the key-notes of the varied harmonies of Paul. His letters only follow where the Gospels lead; and the story embodied in the letters, related unconsciously in allusion, reference, and reminder, we find opened out and definitely stated in the Gospel histories, but precisely the same. Jesus of Nazareth, pre-existent, born of the family of David, come into the world to save sinners, followed by twelve disciples, betrayed, crucified, dead and buried, raised the third day, seen after His resurrection again and again by His disciples, living for evermore, loving, helping still — the "old, old story" stands out as the framework for the Evangelists' narrative, even as it formed the foundation of the letter-writer's arguments.

In order to place before our minds fairly and fully the conditions of the problem we are trying to solve together, it is important to have impressed on our minds this identity between the "fragmentary records" and the regular histories. We all know that as we look onward into Christian literature, the story told in the Gospels is repeated, essentially the same, in all subsequent writings. On the pages of Clement, Ignatius,

Polycarp, Papias, Justin Martyr, Irenæus, Origen, etc., there appear, if not the same words as those of St. Matthew, St. Mark, St. Luke, and St. John, at least words that convey exactly the same account of Christ's life and teaching as they do. No vestige of any other account ever comes before us. There are foolish additions to it and curious theories about it as the years roll past and sects multiply, and human fancy is busy, as usual, in dressing up facts with adornments of fiction. But the one substantial account of the life, death, and resurrection of Jesus has held its ground up to this day. Still the creed of Christian baptism is a simple recital of the main facts told by the Evangelists. We know well the story that has been taught ever since the writers of the Gospels "took in hand to draw up a narrative concerning those matters which have been fulfilled among us, even as they delivered them unto us, which from the beginning were eyewitnesses and ministers of the word."*

The Gospel story has certainly not changed since the Gospels were written. But if we look back further still, can we say the same of its past? If we could get to a more ancient date, nearer to the events described, might we not perceive a

---

* Luke i. 1, 2.

difference? Might we not in the immediate neighbourhood of time and place find a less marvellous story? The "fragmentary records" give a plain answer to such a question. They were certainly written during the lifetime of Christ's companions. They tell the story that evidently had been received and believed years before; they bring us to the very verge of the time when the solemn events were supposed to have taken place. Unchanged as is the Gospel story since the Evangelists put together in order the Apostolic testimony, equally unchanged do we find it to be from the time when Paul embraced the faith he used to persecute.

Those whose mental attitude is such that the narrative of miracle and resurrection is by them "unbelievable," account for the presence of these stories in the Gospels by supposing a long time to have elapsed between Christ's life and the records of it that have reached us. The events, of course, did not occur. The writers of the narrative thought they did; but they wrote long afterwards. The actors in the story, the eyewitnesses of it, were all dead. Years had intervened; and just as the bare rock is soon covered by the lichen, and its sharp outlines rounded by the action of changing seasons, so the story about

Jesus, as His religion spread, came to be adorned by His adherents with an overgrowth of the marvellous; and the plain tale about the good rabbi, teaching a morality in advance of his age and cut off in the midst of his career, killed and buried like any ordinary martyr, was gradually transfigured into the miraculous history now current. For this gradual transfiguration time is required; and, in obedience to the theory, time is made out. The Gospels are at least fifty years younger than is generally supposed. The theory imperatively demands this, and ingenious criticism labours to provide a corresponding supply. Accordingly the Tübingen school push forward the date of the Gospel records, and make time for the original story to expand and develop. But they cannot change the dates of our letters. They are stubborn facts, which no ingenuity can argue away. The letters step back over the imaginary half-century, and certainly date from the lifetime of Christ's contemporaries. Thus the letters not only give their own witness, but ratify and support that of the Gospels. The ground for supposing the Gospels written later than ordinary reason and common-sense would conclude from the way they are mentioned and quoted in ancient literature, is the supposed expansion of their story from a simpler basis. But there is no such simpler basis. Scarcely have the echoes of the cries, "Crucify him; crucify him," died out of the air, when Paul's writings show us that the song of triumph, "Christ is risen," was flying through the world. So the reason for doubting the apostolicity of the Gospels vanishes. The letters that were confessedly written by a contemporary and friend of the Apostles say the same things that the Gospels say.

One history of Christ has been circulated from the very first. The main features have never varied in the telling. It began to be told in Palestine, where Jesus lived, and where Paul was converted. It was told where everything was known about Him Who had been crucified. It was told at the time when all about Him was fresh in men's memories. From this its home centre it spread so rapidly, that when our letters were written communities of believers in Christ had been established in the principal towns and countries in the world. It is the story of our Christian creed. It is the story that, as we learn from Justin Martyr (A.D. 140), used to be recited week by week at the meetings of believers in Christ. It is perfectly certain that Paul believed it to be true. It is perfectly certain that the

Churches to whom he wrote believed it to be true. It is perfectly certain, in short, that a few years after the death of Jesus of Nazareth a conviction as to the facts of His history caused a world-wide revolution in men's thoughts and men's morals.

So far inquirers can still keep side by side, whether they believe the convictions of Christians to be founded on fact or only on delusion. But it is a gain for the cause of truth that we should be led to the very cradle of a belief both in time and place, and that we should be able to say, "Here, at this point, it was that men began to hold such and such convictions." Thus much, at all events, we learn through the letters of "Paul the Apostle:" that when we say, "I believe in Jesus Christ His only Son our Lord, Who suffered under Pontius Pilate, was crucified, dead, and buried; the third day He rose again from the dead; He ascended into heaven, and sitteth at the right hand of God, from whence He shall come to judge the quick and the dead"—that when we say this we only re-echo what was said by numbers of people who lived at the same time and in the same place as Jesus Himself, what they said from the first, what they said in spite of loss, suffering, and peril of death.

CHAPTER XII.

IS THE HISTORY TRUE?

"*Then sawest thou that this fair universe, were it in the meanest province thereof, is indeed the star-domed city of God; that through every star, through every grass-blade, and most through every living soul, the glory of a present God still beams.*"

CARLYLE.

CHAPTER XII.

IS THE HISTORY TRUE?

AND now, as we come to the conclusion of our inquiry, we are better prepared for our last and most important question—Is the old story we have been considering true or not? Let us, even at the risk of repetition, gather up and arrange distinctly in our minds the data we have seen to be supplied to us by Paul's letters. They are briefly as follows :—

Paul was certainly a contemporary of Jesus Christ. The letters we have studied were written during the lifetime of Christ's companions. The convictions expressed in the letters were formed a very few years after Christ's death. They are convictions about facts which he believed had actually taken place, and had taken place publicly a short time before. He had every means of informing himself whether they had really happened or not. He was in frequent communication with men who had lived with Jesus of Nazareth. He spent a considerable time in the place where the events were said to have occurred. He was perfectly convinced that they really had occurred. The companions of Christ with whom he had fellowship shared his conviction. He and they went through great hardship and suffering because they believed it to be their duty to make known those facts to the world. A large number of people in various lands were, within twenty or thirty years of Christ's death, perfectly sure that the story told by Paul and his fellow-labourers about Jesus was true. They also suffered intensely for their faith.

Accompanying Paul's conviction as to certain facts was a wonderful clearness of spiritual insight and elevation of moral sentiment. In the same breath he propagated holiness of life and belief in Jesus. Though he was warm and earnest, he was manifestly gifted with strong common-sense, clearness of judgment, and practical sagacity. It was in pressing upon men's consciences the claims of a lofty righteousness that he showed upon the pages of the letters his convictions as to the events of Christ's life. Those to whom he wrote disagreed with him in many things; some of them opposed him very bitterly; but they all agreed in the belief he held that Jesus Christ lived a supernatural life, died, and rose again. On this foundation of belief in certain definite facts was reared that great edifice which we call the Christian Church. Its creed, its organisation, its teaching, its Sacraments, we see in these old letters, the same essentially as they are to-day, all founded on the story of fact which Paul believed, which Christ's Apostles and companions believed, which the whole community believed, and for which they endured loss, persecution, labour, and even death.

Is this story of facts then about Jesus Christ, so intensely, so passionately believed by His own contemporaries, true or false? It is a beautiful story, the account of a stately life lived amidst lowly surroundings, but so noble, so loving, so self-devoted, that the thought and moral feeling of the world has been lit up by it ever since. The telling of it has brought comfort and rest to millions of troubled hearts through the passing centuries. The remembrance of it has given strength for righteousness from generation to generation, courage and joy amidst difficulties, temptation, and trial to those who have been striving to live for goodness. All the grandest efforts for the elevation of humanity and for the relief of its sufferings have, more or less, sprung from the motives this history has supplied. It is certainly beautiful. It is a blessing to the world. It has given us martyrs, confessors, preachers, philosophers, philanthropists. It has been re-echoed in the world's noblest poems, reflected in its fairest pictures, built up in the marble of its most solemn cathedrals. It is told daily by mothers to the children at their knees, it is lisped by infant voices, sung beside watch-fires on battle-fields, gasped out with gratitude and triumph by the failing breath of dying men and women. The same story still, the same in its essence, unspoiled amidst human follies, fables, exaggerations, superstitions, bigotry, and fanaticism; still the great story that Paul believed, and St. Augustine, and St. Francis d'Assisi, and Thomas à Kempis, and Xavier, and Savonarola, and Luther, and Wesley, and Whitefield, and Fenelon, and Washington, and Wilberforce, and Sir Isaac Newton, and General Gordon; this same story has come down to us unchanged from the time and place where Jesus lived. Is it true, or is it false? True or false the issue must be. For we have not to deal, as we have seen, with a developed story or a story taken up and transfigured by the myths of centuries, but with one definite narrative of fact, told exactly the same when the tears were hardly dry for the death of Jesus as it is told to-day. Is the story true, or is it a lie or a dream?

If it were an ordinary story, no one would for a moment doubt its veracity. There are few historical events on record attested by such clear evidence. Contemporary witness, agreement of successive writers, marks of truthfulness and ingenuousness in the historians' language, a long train of momentous consequences following the facts, public institutions growing out of them and existing till this day—all kinds of evidence that we look upon as valuable in proof of long-past events are heaped together here. No ordinary event related to us with such corroboration would ever be doubted. Why are there doubts felt as to this history? Because the events related are not ordinary. If they really occurred, they imply what is called "the supernatural." No known force could have produced the miracles and resurrection of Jesus Christ. To believe them would involve believing in some Power beyond what is generally termed the power of "nature." And many thinkers have been led by their studies of the phenomena within their reach to believe that the "supernatural" is impossible, "unthinkable." They have only one thing to do therefore with all the evidence about the life of Jesus: not to weigh it, not to dwell upon it and work it out in their minds, not to judge of it with careful and discriminating judgment—only one thing: just to see where the flaw in it can be. Flaw there *must* be somewhere. The conclusion being impossible, the premisses must be wrong. The whole effort of whatever thought they give it is to suggest some method by which the apparently strong evidence may be explained away.

I do not think this tone of mind is fair, or truly philosophical; but I am obliged to confess that to a great degree I sympathise with it. I feel that there is a tremendous difficulty in really believing "the supernatural." Whenever I hear any story that even remotely involves supernatural agency, I instinctively, and without any consideration, feel inclined to reject it. No matter what may be said about it, I feel sure it cannot be true. This, however, is only a feeling, not a verdict of the understanding. When I look for the reason of the feeling, I do not find that it bears the crucible of careful investigation. The blind resistance comes rather from a mental *habit*, than from deliberately formed conviction. There is a sluggishness in the intellectual powers that makes it hard for them to take in and give due value to unusual classes of phenomena.* I hear, for example, a good deal in the present day of occult and subtle "psychical forces." I hear descriptions of curious phenomena under such names as "mesmerism," "spiritualism," "trance," "second sight," etc. My instinctive feeling is at once to relegate them all to the class of "unbelievable" things. I am disinclined to weigh the evidence for them with any care. I turn away from them with a kind of impatience, as delusions which it is waste of time seriously to discuss. But such a frame of mind, I know, is unreasonable. My instinct prompts me to it, but my understanding reproaches me for it. Impulse says, "Reject summarily. Be sure that the supposed evidence is only fraud or folly." Reason remonstrates, "This unwillingness is, in the strictest sense of the word, *prejudice*, judging before the grounds for judging are present to the mind." Phenomena that I am disposed to dismiss as on the face of them incredible I find spoken of by

---

* This sluggishness is well illustrated by Mr. J. S. Mill's remarks on the resistance offered to the Newtonian theory as to bodies acting upon each other though separated by enormous distances: "The temporary difficulty found in apprehending any action of body upon body unlike what people were accustomed to created a natural prejudice, which was long a serious impediment to the reception of the Newtonian theory" ("Examination of Sir W. Hamilton's Philosophy," p. 547).

one of our most thoughtful leaders of public opinion in the following terms : " The truth certainly is that the longer the phenomena of mesmerism, trance, and the less ordinary psychical states are examined, the more certain it is, on evidence that no candid mind can reject, that even in this life there is something in man which can occasionally pass beyond the limits of sense ; and that after death there are in cases, relatively rare but collectively very numerous, phenomena which are not to be explained at all unless they can be explained as manifestations of a still existent personality."[*] Whether this conclusion is correct or incorrect, I feel that, in presence of the evidence on the subject collected by dispassionate observers, the mental attitude I am naturally disposed to take up towards it is an unreasonable attitude. Our instincts have most important functions, but they must always be kept under the control of reason, experience, and the moral sense, or they become dangerous and headstrong tyrants. We must guard against this tyranny. If I say to myself, " I am certain that everything 'supernatural' is impossible," I am yielding to an instinctive tendency, strengthened by habits of observation

---

[*] *Spectator*, January 22nd, 1887.

in one direction; but I am not following any deduction of widely exercised reason. Am I not submitting to a tyranny? It is hardly necessary to observe that such words as *natural, supernatural,* and *invariable law* are full of ambiguity, and might easily become blind instruments to carry on the blind tyranny. If by "nature" I mean the whole sum of existing things, including the Power, whatever it be, that brought them into existence, then nothing can be supernatural. Events that we call supernatural are but the exercise of nature's forces in ways of which we have but few examples, and whose movement we have not faculties to analyse. If by nature I mean only the action and interaction of particles of matter, then to say that there can be the "supernatural" is only to say that there may be something else in the universe besides matter. When I speak of "*law,*" I only use an abstract term expressing the constancy with which certain phenomena are observed to follow each other. If I suppose that natural law has any binding power to forbid unusual occurrences or to prevent new or previously unobserved causes from producing new or previously unobserved effects, I am endowing a mental abstraction with an authority altogether imaginary.

The more I study "Nature," the more I feel her mystery and wonder. Her simplest processes are inscrutable. The mutual attraction and repulsion of particles of matter; light, heat, and electricity; the phenomena of chemical affinity alike on earth and in distant stars; life, growth, reproduction—what wonders are implied in them all! When we have observed what we call the laws of their action and described some of them under scientific formulæ, have we come nearer the mystery of their being? "Who knoweth the way of the spirit," says the wise man of old, "or how the bones do grow in the womb of her that is with child?" Can we answer as to that "*how*" at all more distinctly to-day? There are a few scarcely distinguishable particles of "protoplasm;" one, by the mystic force of *natura naturans*, develops into a limpet clinging to the rock, another into a soaring eagle, another into a warhorse, "whose neck is clothed with thunder," "the glory of whose nostrils is terrible." Can any science explain the inscrutable process? Our study of evolution may show us interesting steps in Nature's working, but does it bring us any nearer to the secrets of her heart? And when we think of our own selves, our consciousness, will, reason, moral sense, hopes, longings, aspirations, whether we consider these results to be only produced by movements in the molecules of brain-matter, or believe there is a "something" within us, above and beyond matter, that uses the matter of brain and nerve and muscle as its instrument, equally we feel that we are "fearfully and wonderfully made," and that every blush upon the cheek, every tear dimming the eye, every heart-throb of hope or fear or grief, has its source in depths that our understanding cannot fathom. We cannot help feeling from time to time as we ponder all this

>   "A sense sublime
> Of something far more deeply interfused,
> Whose dwelling is the light of setting suns,
> And the round ocean, and the living air,
> And the blue sky, and in the mind of man,
> A motion and a spirit that impels
> All thinking things, all objects of all thought,
> And rolls through all things ; "*

and conscious of this marvel and mystery in ourselves and all around us, the word *supernatural* ceases to be a bugbear to us. The story of Jesus Christ is wonderful and beautiful ; whether we are to call it "supernatural" is only a question of words. It is certainly different from anything that has come within the range of human experience

---

* Wordsworth : " Lines on Tintern Abbey."

before or since. It is *unique;* if it were not so, it would have lost its glorious significance, and would not be worth contending about. But it would be strange philosophy to suppose that what is unique within the narrow limits of our experience is therefore impossible. And, taken in connection with mental and moral phenomena, the miracles and resurrection of Jesus may well be reducible under some wide and holy law. They are unique, but neither isolated nor monstrous. They are in harmony with the highest ideas of mind and soul and spirit; they are in harmony with the ethical welfare of the human race. This is evident from experience; for where they have been most firmly believed there have been the noblest action and the happiest and most peaceful living.

Is the story true, then? We come back upon this question, which is the really essential one to consider. We must fix our attention upon the evidence. We must weigh it and sift it. It should be strong and clear to lead us to such unusual, such momentous conclusions. We must not say that no evidence will persuade us; if we do, we are weakly yielding to a habit of the mind, a mechanical impulse, instead of using scientific investigation. One of the disciples of

Jesus described in the old Gospel history made a statement of the kind. When Christ's other companions declared that they had seen Him risen, Thomas said that he would not and could not believe unless he actually could put his fingers into the print of the nails that had fastened Him to the Cross. That incredulity was not philosophical, but the result of habit, prejudice, and perhaps a morbid and desponding disposition. If ever I am inclined to similar doubting, if the thought comes pressing upon me unbidden, "The supernatural is impossible," I believe it would be unreasonable weakness to yield to the impulse, as I do not know what the supernatural is, and have no means of judging as to its impossibility.

But there are classes of phenomena which do come under the range of my experience, and with regard to which I am capable of judging as to their possibility or impossibility. And when I think of the evidence before my reason and conscience for the story of the crucified and risen Jesus, I feel it is impossible that such evidence could mislead. That the character of Jesus should have been invented by dishonest forgers or fanatical dreamers is, I am quite sure, impossible. That Paul and His other Apostles should have preached their noble, large-minded, and holy doctrines while they were propagating what they believed to be untrue is impossible. That they should all have imagined Jesus to be alive while He was still mouldering in His grave under their feet is impossible. That they should have had their lifelong Jewish prejudices overcome, all their narrow-minded ideas swept away, all their earthly desires and longings crushed, by their deference to One Whose life was a wild dream or a daring imposture, is impossible. That His companions, who loved Him, and lived with Him, and spent years in His society, should have been mistaken on the plain issue as to whether He did or did not do the things the writer of our letters and His other disciples said He did, is impossible. That He could have taught as He did, that they could have taught as they did, if He and they were the victims of an absurd delusion, is impossible. That there could be any kind of glamour, or enthusiasm, or sentimental imagining that would make a number of men think that a series of events happened within their experience which never had happened, and as they taught them teach at the same time the plainest, most sensible, as well as most beautiful morality, and be so sure they had seen things they never saw that they should let themselves be killed rather than cease to declare they had witnessed them—such delusion and such conduct my judgment unhesitatingly declares to be impossible.

When I think of all this, of all the evidence history gives, all the evidence my heart responds to in every fibre, as to the unique and glorious life of Jesus of Nazareth, I leave my attitude of inquiry. I have been inquiring and searching, but not in vain. I have found what I wanted. I have found a real religion. I have found a narrative of outward facts which the verdict of my understanding declares to be true. I have found a revelation from the great unseen God thrilling to my heart and conscience, satisfying my longings, strengthening me for the battle against evil, assuring me of the reality of righteousness, pointing me to a Father above Who loves me, to a Saviour Who forgives me, to a Divine Spirit Who comes and dwells in my heart and gives me a power for goodness sufficient for my needs. So I can live my life bravely. I have an object worth living for. The doing of duty to-day is the beginning of an eternal career of interesting service. My earthly friends and companions are bound to me by a tie that death is not to loose. We have a "Father's house" beyond the grave. The calamities of life cannot crush, nor the troubles and toils of life overshadow, our joy and hope. There is a Providence that "makes all things work together for good." "Verily there is a reward for the righteous; doubtless there is a God that judgeth the earth." Though doubts may sometimes cloud our faith, though the "changes and chances of life" may sometimes make the tears "rise in the heart and gather to the eyes," though efforts for the right are often only imperfectly successful, yet we can still have ringing in our ears the cheery note of our old letter-writer, "Be steadfast, unmovable, always abounding in the work of the Lord, forasmuch as ye know that your labour is not in vain in the Lord." And beyond this voice we can hear the echo of another grander and sweeter still : "Let not your heart be troubled. Ye believe in God ; believe also in me."

THE END.

Printed by Hazell, Watson, & Viney, Ld., London and Aylesbury.

www.ingramcontent.com/pod-product-compliance
Lightning Source LLC
Chambersburg PA
CBHW030320170426
43202CB00009B/1088